Favorite Recipes From the Heart of Amish Country

Compiled by:

Rachel Miller
862 SR 93 NW
Sugarcreek, Ohio 44681

Copyright ©1995
All rights reserved.

First Printing - 1995
Second Printing - 1996
Third Printing - 1998

Typeset and printed by:

SCHLABACH PRINTERS

2881 State Route 93 ● Sugarcreek, Ohio 44681
(216) 852-4687 ● Fax (216) 852-2689

Introduction

Recipes in this cook book are mostly from relatives, friends, and neighbors. Other recipes were contributed by family members and from Mom's collection of recipes she has used over the years. I also included some of my own favorites.

Table, chairs, china, and china cabinet on the cover are a few of the heirlooms that are still in the family.

I would like to thank everyone who contributed recipes and helped make this cookbook a possibility. Also a special thanks to Jake Mast who photographed the cover picture.

Recipes compiled by Rachel Miller

Abbreviations

Tbsp. = Tablespoon
tsp. = teaspoon
gal. = gallon
doz. = dozen
qt. = quart
pt. = pint
lb. = pound
oz. = ounce
c. = cup
pkg. = package

lg. = large
sm. = small
med. = medium
sq. = square
approx. = approximately
min. = minute
hr. = hour
choc. = chocolate
env. = envelope

Equivalents

1 Tbsp. = 3 tsp.
2 Tbsp. = 1 oz.
1/4 c. = 4 Tbsp.
1/3 c. = 5 Tbsp. plus 1 tsp.
1/2 c. = 8 Tbsp.
7/8 c. = 14 Tbsp.

1 lb. flour = 4 c. (all-purpose)
1 lb. granulated sugar = 2 c.
1 lb. rice = 2 c.

1 fluid oz. - 2 Tbsp.
1 lb. confectioner's sugar = 3 1/2 c. sifted

3 oz. jello = 1/3 c.
3 oz. instant pudding = 1/2 c.

1 pint = 2 c.
1 quart = 4 c.
1 liter = 4 c. plus 3 Tbsp.
1 oz. (dry) = 2 Tbsp.
16 ounce = 1 lb.

1 lb. raisins = 3 c.
1 lb. cornmeal = 3 c.

1 lb. brown sugar = 2 1/4 c.

1 pkg. yeast = 1 Tbsp.
1 pkg. unflavored gelatin = 1 Tbsp.

Substitutions

1 c. sour cream = 7/8 c. sour milk plus 3 Tbsp. butter

1 tsp. shredded lemon peel = 1/2 tsp. lemon extract

1 Tbsp. cornstarch = 2 Tbsp. flour

1 c. corn syrup = 1 c. granulated sugar plus 1/4 c. liquid

2 c. tomato sauce − 3/4 c. tomato paste plus 1 c. water

1 med. onion = 2 Tbsp. instant minced onion or 1 tsp. onion powder

1 tsp. baking powder = 1/4 tsp. soda plus 1/2 tsp. cream of tartar

1 c. sifted all purpose flour = 1 c. plus 2 Tbsp. sifted cake flour

1 oz. square chocolate = 3 to 4 Tbsp. cocoa plus 1 tsp. shortening

1 c. honey = 1 to 1 1/4 c. sugar plus 1/4 c. liquid or 1 c. molasses

1 c. sweet milk = 1 c. sour milk or buttermilk plus 1/2 tsp. soda

1 c. sour milk = 1 c. sweet milk plus 1 Tbsp. vinegar or lemon juice

1 c. buttermilk = 1 c. sour milk or 1 c. yogurt

1 c. light cream = 7/8 c. skim milk plus 3 Tbsp. butter

1 c. heavy cream = 3/4 c. skim milk plus 1/3 c. butter

Kitchen Hints

If soup is too salty place a raw potato in the soup and it will absorb the salt.

When making mashed potatoes add chicken broth with milk to enhance their flavor.

Rinse saucepan with water before heating milk to keep it from scorching so quickly.

To keep cookies soft, place a fresh slice of bread in cookie container.

Put meatballs in refrigerator for 20 min. before frying and they won't fall apart.

When cream will not whip, add an egg white to your cream. Chill, and it will whip.

Before frosting an angel food cake, chill the cake in refrigerator. Frosting goes on easy with no mess.

A teaspoon of baking powder in the water which meat or vegetables are cooked will help make them tender.

Add 1/8 teaspoon of baking powder to frosting to keep it from becoming sugary. Also helps keep it fluffy.

A fresh egg sinks in water and lies on it's side. If it stands on end it's getting old. If it floats get rid of it.

Place a piece of bread in brown sugar container and sugar will stay soft.

Store popcorn in refrigerator until just before you're ready to pop it. Most kernels will pop.

After rice has been cooked and drained, place a slice of dry bread on top of rice and cover. Bread will absorb the moisture and rice will be dry and fluffy.

When baking bread place a small dish of water in the oven to keep the crust from getting too hard.

To prevent your cookbook from getting spills and splatters on while cooking, slide it into a gallon size freezer bag. Press out the extra air and zip the bag closed.

To remove labels that are stuck on glass jars, briskly rub on mayonnaise then soak the jar in warm water. The label will peel off easily.

To prevent onions from burning your eyes, hold them under water while peeling and slicing.

Substitute 1/2 of milk for leftover coffee next time you bake a chocolate pie to give it more flavor.

To make a fertilizer for plants, save egg shells. Soak them in water for a couple days then use the water for the plants.

To prevent silver from tarnishing keep a piece of alum in the silverware drawer.

To bleach handkerckiefs, towels and etc., soak overnight in a solution of 1/2 tsp. cream of tartar to each qt. of water.

Beat an egg yolk with a tsp. of cold water and spread over pie crust before baking to get a rich brown crust.

To bake potatoes; wrap in foil and bake in muffin tins.

Add one tablespoon of flour for each cup of sugar when making fudge. Fudge will not get sugary.

Table of Contents

Appetizers, Beverages, and Dips 7

Breakfast 15

Bread, Rolls, and Pastries 27

Main Dishes and Vegetables 39

Soups, Salads, and Dressings 75

Desserts 93

Cakes and Frostings 119

Pies 145

Cookies 165

Snacks and Misc. 197

Appetizers, Beverages, and Dips

CHEESE BALL

2 (8 oz.) pkgs. cream cheese
1 Tbsp. onion
1 Tbsp. dried parsley flakes
1 tsp. real lemon juice
4 oz. pkg. shredded cheddar cheese
2 Tbsp. Worcestershire sauce
dried chipped beef (cut in fine pieces)

CHEESE BALL

2 (8 oz.) pkgs. cream cheese
2 c. chopped pecans
1 Tbsp. seasoned salt
8 1/2 oz. can crushed pineapples, drained
2 Tbsp. chopped onion

Soften cream cheese, gradually stir in pineapple, 1 c. pecans, onion, and salt. Chill well. Form in ball and roll in remaining pecans.

CRUNCHY SWISS AND HAM APPETIZERS

2 c. stiff mashed potatoes
2 c. chopped ham, cooked
1 c. shredded Swiss cheese
1/3 c. mayonnaise
1/4 c. minced onion
1 egg, well beaten
1 tsp. prepared mustard
1/2 tsp. salt
1/4 tsp. pepper
3 1/2 c. cornflakes, crushed

Combine all ingredients except cornflakes. Chill. Shape into 1" balls and roll in cornflakes. Place on greased cookie sheets and bake at 350° for 30 min. Yield: about 4 doz. NOTE: A delicious way to use leftover mashed potatoes.

FRUIT SLUSH

2 c. sugar
6 oz. can orange juice concentrate
3 c. water
2 bananas

20 oz. can crushed pineapple

Mix sugar and water till sugar is dissolved. Cool. Mix orange juice as directed on can. Add mashed bananas and stir in pineapple. Any other fruit is optional. Freeze in individual cups. Allow to thaw till slushy before serving.

SLUSH DRINK

6 bananas, mashed
2 cans pineapple juice
1 can frozen orange juice, diluted
4 c. sugar
6 c. water
2 - 2 liters 7-Up

Heat water and sugar to dissolve sugar. Add to rest of ingredients. Freeze. Just before serving add 7-Up. Should be thawed and a little slushy.

Mrs. Martha Schlabach, Mrs. Mary Ellen Wengerd

GOLDEN PUNCH

46 oz. pineapple juice
6 oz. can frozen orange juice
6 oz. can frozen lemonade
2 qt. 7-Up

Prepare lemonade and orange juice according to directions on can. Add to pineapple juice. Add 7-Up just before serving.

Mrs. Mabel Yoder

PARTY PUNCH

1 pkg. cherry Kool-Aid
1 pkg. strawberry Kool-Aid
6 oz. frozen orange juice
6 oz. frozen lemonade
2 c. sugar
3 qts. water
2 c. ginger ale or 7-Up

Add 7-Up or ginger ale just before serving.

Ruby Beachy, Barbara Jean Mullet

ORANGE SHERBET PUNCH

2 pkg. orange Kool-Aid
2 c. sugar
1 gal. water
12 oz. can frozen orange juice concentrate
1 qt. 7-Up
1/2 gal. orange sherbet

Mix all ingredients except sherbet and 7-Up. Add 7-Up and sherbet just before serving. Drop sherbet in punch with ice cream scoop.

BEST EVER PUNCH

1 can pineapple juice
2 pkgs. lemon-lime Kool-Aid
1 qt. lime sherbet
7-Up

Mix all ingredients, adding sherbet last. Scoop sherbet in drink with ice cream scoop.

HOT CHOCOLATE MIX

6 c. powdered milk
1 lb. Nestle's Quick
8 oz. coffee mate
1/2 c. powdered sugar

Mix well. Store in a air tight container. Mix 1/3 c. to every cup of water.

Mrs. Mary Ann Hershberger

WARM TACO DIP

1 lb. hamburger
2 lbs. Velveeta cheese
1 can tomato soup
1 can mushroom soup
1 can Nacho cheese soup
2 med. onions, diced
1 tsp. ea. pepper, onion powder, garlic salt and worcestershire sauce

Brown hamburger with onions. Put everything in a crockpot and heat, or heat on top of stove till cheese is melted. Serve warm.

Mrs. Ora Lena Miller

HAMBURGER CHEESE DIP

1 lb. hamburger
1 can tomato soup
1 tsp. chili powder
1/2 tsp. garlic powder
1 lb. velveeta cheese
1 can mushroom soup
1 tsp. Worcestershire sauce
1 c. peppers

Heat until cheese is melted. Serve warm with doritoes.

Ruby Beachy

CHEESE DIP

14 oz. Pimento cheese spread
8 oz. cream cheese
6 oz. cheddar cheese spread
1/2 tsp. garlic powder
1/2 tsp. onion powder
1 tsp. chopped parsley (fine)
1 Tbsp. skim milk or till right consistency
horseradish to taste

~ The only thing people do that doesn't get better with practice is getting up in the morning. ~

CITRUS DIP

1/2 c. orange juice
1 c. white sugar
1 egg, beaten
1 Tbsp. grated orange rind, optional

Cook over low heat for around 6 min. Cool thoroughly. Fold in 1 1/2 c. whipped topping and 8 oz. cream cheese. Chill. Serve with fresh fruit.

Mrs. (Henry) Edna Miller

FRUIT DIP

8 oz. cream cheese
7 oz. marshmallow topping
1 sm. container cool whip

Add pineapple juice till dipping consistency.

Mrs. Esta Miller

FRESH FRUIT DIP

1 container strawberry yogurt
1 sm. container cool whip
1 small jar marshmallow topping

Beat together and dip!

Mrs. Ada Mullet

FRUIT DIP

13 oz. jar Kraft marshmallow creme
8 oz. cream cheese
1 Tbsp. lemon or orange juice

Mix ingredients well. Chill.

Ruth Ann Miller

TAFFY APPLE DIP

8 oz. cream cheese, softened
3/4 c. packed brown sugar
1 Tbsp. vanilla extract
1/2 c. chopped nuts
6 apples, cut in wedges

In a small bowl, beat cream cheese, brown sugar, and vanilla until smooth. Spread mixture on a small serving plate; top with nuts and serve with apple wedges.

Barbara Jean Mullet

VEGETABLE DIP

1 c. mayonnaise
1 c. sour cream
1 Tbsp. dry onion flakes
1 Tbsp. parsley flakes

1 tsp. dill weed
1/2 tsp. accent
1/2 tsp. worcestershire sauce
1 tsp. Lawry's seasoned salt

Mix all ingredients together and chill for several hours. Serve with vegetables or snacks.

SALSA

2 qts. tomatoes
3 green peppers
6 hot pepppers
1 c. onions
3 to 4 garlic cloves

2 Tbsp. white sugar
2 Tbsp. salt
1 c. vinegar
2 Tbsp. clear jel

Cook for 45 min. Add clear jel about the last 10 min. Yield: 4 pt.

Barbara Troyer

My Favorite Recipes:

My Favorite Recipes:

Breakfast

ONION CAKE

3 bacon strips, diced
4 onions, finely chopped
3 Tbsp. butter or margarine
1/2 c. sour cream
1 Tbsp. all-purpose flour
1/2 tsp. salt
3 eggs, beaten
8 oz. refrigerated crescent rolls

Fry bacon until crisp. Drain. In same skillet cook onions in butter until tender. Cool. In a bowl combine sour cream, flour, and salt, add eggs. Stir in bacon and onions, set aside. Separate crescent roll dough into 4 rectangles. Pat dough into the bottom and 1" up the sides of a greased 9" square baking pan, stretching as needed and pinching edges together to seal. Pour onion mixture over dough. Bake at 375° for 30 min. or until topping is set and crust is golden. Cool slightly before cutting. Serve warm. Yield: 16 servings.

SHEEP HERDERS BREAKFAST

1 lb. bacon, diced
1 med. onion, chopped
32 oz. frozen hash brown potatoes, thawed
10 eggs
salt and pepper
2 c. cheddar cheese, shredded
fresh parsley (optional)

In large skillet fry bacon and onions until bacon is crisp. Drain all but 1/2 of drippings. Add hash browns to skillet. Mix well. Cook over med. heat for 10 min. turning when browned. Make 10 wells evenly spaced in the hash browns; place 1 egg in each well. Sprinkle with salt, pepper and cheese. Cover and cook over low heat for about 10 min. or until eggs are set. Garnish with parsley. Serve immediately. Yield: 10 servings.

Mrs. Mary Ellen Wengerd

HAM AND CHEESE OMELET

1 c. milk
8 eggs
1/2 tsp. seasoned salt
3 oz. meat, any kind, cut up
1 c. cheddar cheese, shredded
3 Tbsp. chopped onion

Beat together eggs, milk, and salt. Add remaining ingredients. Pour into a cake pan. Bake uncovered at 325° for 40 to 45 min.

Anita Troyer

BREAKFAST CASSEROLE

2 lbs. sausage	6 slices bread, cubed
8 eggs	1 c. shredded cheese
2 c. milk	1 can cream of
1 tsp. salt	mushroom soup

Brown sausage, drain. Add soup. Put bread in bottom of pan. Beat eggs, add the rest of ingredients. Pour over bread then spread sausage on top. Cover and refrigerate overnight. Bake uncovered at 350° for about 1 hr.

Linda Miller

BREAKFAST CASSEROLE

Beat 6 eggs, and add any kind of pork, ham, sausage, or bacon. Add onion, salt, pepper, 2 c. milk and 6 slices bread in crumbs.

Pour into greased cake pan and refrigerate overnite. Bake at 350° for 1/2 hr. Top with cheese then melt cheese.

Mrs. Joan Mast, Mary Anna Troyer

BREAKFAST PIZZA

1 1/2 cans crescent rolls	6 strips bacon, fried
1 can mushroom soup	2 scrambled eggs, optional
1/2 lb. sausage, browned	1 lg. potato, shredded
1/2 lb. hamburger, browned	& cooked
ham, diced	Mozzarella cheese, shredded

Thin soup with a little milk. Put on crescent rolls in order given. Bake at 350° for 1/2 hr. Yield: 1 pan.

Mrs. Nettie Miller

~ Some people grow under responsibility, others merely swell. ~

FEATHER-LIGHT MUFFINS

1/3 c. shortening	1 1/2 tsp. baking powder
1/2 c. sugar	1/2 tsp. salt
1 egg	1/4 tsp. ground nutmeg
1 1/2 c. cake flour	1/2 c. milk

TOPPING:

1/2 c. sugar	1 tsp. ground cinnamon
1/2 c. butter or margarine, melted	

In a mixing bowl, cream shortening, sugar, and egg. Combine dry ingredients. Add to creamed mixture alternately with milk. Fill greased muffin tins 2/3 full. Bake at 325° for 20 to 25 min. or until golden brown. Let cool for 3 to 4 min. Meanwhile combine sugar and cinnamon. Roll warm muffins in melted butter, then in sugar mixture. Serve warm. Yield: 8 to 10 muffins.

ORANGE CORN MUFFINS

1 c. yellow cornmeal	1 egg, beaten
1 c. all-purpose flour	1 c. milk
1/3 c. sugar	1/4 c. vegetable oil
4 tsp. baking powder	1 Tbsp. grated orange peel
1/4 tsp. salt	

Combine cornmeal, flour, sugar, baking powder and salt. In a seperate bowl combine egg, milk, oil, and orange peel. Add to cornmeal mixture, stirring just until ingredients are combined. Fill greased muffin tins 2/3 full. Bake at 425° for around 15 min.

OATMEAL APPLE RAISIN MUFFINS

1 c. flour	1 tsp. salt
1 c. quick oats	1 tsp. nutmeg
1/3 c. sugar	3/4 c. milk
1 Tbsp. baking powder	1/2 c. vegetable oil
2 tsp. cinnamon	1 egg

Sift together, flour, oats, sugar, baking powder, cinnamon, salt, and nutmeg. Beat together the milk, oil, and egg. Add liquid mixture to dry ingredients,stirring just to moisten. Gently fold in 1 apple, peeled and finely chopped. Add 1 c. raisins. Fill 12 greased muffin cups 3/4 full. Bake at 400° for 15 to 20 min.

Mrs. Joan Mast

GRANDMA'S APPLE MUFFINS

1 1/2 c. flour	1 c. chopped apple
1 c. sugar	1/2 c. chopped walnuts
2 tsp. baking powder	2 eggs
2 tsp. cinnamon	1/2 c. buttermilk
1 tsp. baking soda	1/2 c. margarine, melted
1/2 tsp. cloves	

STREUSEL TOPPING:

1/2 c. flour	1 tsp. cinnamon
1/3 c. packed brown sugar	1/4 c. margarine, melted

Mix in a small bowl and set aside. For muffins; mix flour, sugar, baking powder, cinnamon, soda and cloves in a large bowl. Add apples and walnuts. Toss to coat. In a small bowl beat eggs with a fork, beat in buttermilk and margarine. Add to flour mixture, stir until just blended. Fill greased pans 2/3 full. Sprinkle with streusel topping. Bake in a preheated 400° oven for 15 to 25 minutes.

BLUEBERRY OAT MUFFINS

1 c. oats   1 c. sour milk
   Combine and let set.
1 egg, beaten   1/4 c. melted butter
   Add to oats mixture.
1 c. flour   1/2 tsp. salt
3/4 c. brown sugar 1/2 tsp. soda
1 tsp. baking powder

Mix everything together. Stir just enough till all is moistened. Fold in 1 cup blueberries, fresh or frozen. Bake at 400° for 15 to 20 min.

Linda Miller

~ *When you are right, no one remembers. When you are wrong, no one forgets.* ~

CHEESE MUFFINS

2 c. flour
2 1/2 c. baking powder
1/2 tsp. salt
1/2 c. grated cheese

1 egg
1 c. milk
4 Tbsp. shortening, melted
1/2 tsp. paprika

Mix flour, baking powder, salt, paprika, and cheese in a bowl. In a separate bowl, beat one egg, then add milk and shortening. Combine mixtures by stirring only enough to mix. Batter will look rough. Fill lightly greased muffin cups 2/3 full. Bake in a preheated 400° oven for 20 to 25 minutes.

BRAN BISCUITS

2 eggs, beaten
1/3 c. milk
1 c. bran flakes
1/2 c. flour
1/2 c. whole wheat flour

2 Tbsp. brown sugar
1 Tbsp. baking powder
1/4 tsp. salt
1/4 c. shortening

Combine eggs, milk and crushed bran flakes. Let stand for 5 min. Meanwhile, in a mixing bowl, stir together flours, brown sugar, baking powder, and salt. Cut in shortening until mixture resembles coarse crumbs. Make a well in center, add bran mixture all at once to dry mixture. Stir just until dough clings together. Knead gently on floured surface, 12 to 15 strokes. Roll out dough and cut out with biscuit cutter or floured glass. Place on an ungreased baking sheet. Bake at 450° for 8 to 10 minutes.

BEST EVER BISCUITS

2 c. flour
2 tsp. sugar
1/2 tsp. salt
2/3 c. milk

4 tsp. baking powder
1/2 tsp. cream of tartar
1/2 c. shortening

Combine all the ingredients. Bake at 350°.

BUTTERMILK BISCUITS

2 c. minus 2 Tbsp. flour	1/4 tsp. soda
2 1/2 tsp. baking powder	1/3 c. shortening or lard
1 tsp. salt	3/4 c. buttermilk

Mix dry ingredients, add shortening and mix. Then add buttermilk. Roll and cut. Bake at 400° for 20 minutes.

PANCAKES

1 egg, separated	1 Tbsp. sugar
1 c. buttermilk	1 tsp. baking powder
2 Tbsp. liquid shortening	1/2 tsp. soda
1 c. flour	1/2 tsp. salt

Mix all ingredients together except for egg white. Beat egg white and fold in last.

Mrs. Margaret Yoder

PANCAKES

3 c. flour	3 tsp. baking powder
3 eggs, separated	3 Tbsp. sugar
3 c. milk	pinch of salt

Mix flour, sugar, salt, and baking powder together. Beat egg yolks with milk, then add to flour mixture. Beat egg whites until stiff and fold in last. THE BEST!

Ruby Beachy

PANCAKES

2 c. flour	1 tsp. soda
2 Tbsp. whole wheat flour	2 eggs
salt	1 Tbsp. lard, melted
2 tsp. baking powder	

Add milk till right consistency.

Mrs. Martha Schlabach

~ *Success comes in cans -*
I can, you can, we can. ~

LIGHT PANCAKES

Combine:
1 beaten egg	7 oz. milk
1/8 c. vinegar	1/8 c. vegetable oil

Add:
1 c. flour	1 1/2 Tbsp. sugar
1/2 tsp. soda	1/2 tsp. salt

Mix or beat until smooth. Yield: 10 pancakes.

Mrs. (Henry) Edna Miller

POTATO PANCAKES

4 c. shredded potatoes	1 tsp. salt
1 egg, beaten	1/4 tsp. pepper
3 Tbsp. all-purpose flour	cooking oil
1 Tbsp. grated onion	

Place potatoes in a large bowl. Add egg, flour, onion, salt, and pepper. Mix well. Heat oil in a skillet over medium heat. Drop by 1/3 cups full into hot oil. Flatten to form a pancake. Fry until golden brown on both sides. Drain on a paper towel. Serve immediately. Yield: 6 servings.

Mrs. Ada Troyer

FRENCH TOAST

1 egg	4 slices bread
1/2 tsp. cinnamon	1/3 c. milk

Blend all ingredients except bread. Dip bread slices in egg mixture. Fry in butter until golden brown. Top with maple syrup.

Mrs. Sue Miller

GRAPENUTS

3 1/4 c. brown sugar	6 Tbsp. oleo, melted
6 c. whole wheat flour	1/2 tsp. maple flavoring
1 tsp. salt	1/2 Tbsp. vanilla
1/2 Tbsp. soda	2 1/2 c. sour milk or buttermilk

Mix sugar, flour and salt. Set aside. Add soda to milk then to flour mixture. Mix flavoring with oleo then mix everything together. Mix well. Bake in sheet cake pan at 350° until done. Crumble and dry. I use salad master to crumble. Drying in 100° oven overnite is easy. Be sure to leave oven door open a crack.

Mrs. Miriam Troyer

DELUXE HONEY NUT GRANOLA

10 c. oatmeal	1 1/3 c. honey
2 c. brown sugar	1 1/3 c. oleo, melted
2 c. coconut or sunflower seeds	2 1/2 tsp. cinnamon
1 c. wheat germ	4 tsp. vanilla
1 c. water	1 c. each of raisins, dates, or chopped dried fruit

Preheat oven to 250°. Combine all ingredients, except for fruit. Bake 45 minutes to 1 hour. Do not stir. Spread out to cool. Add fruit. You can use peanut butter and not as much sugar.

SAUSAGE GRAVY

1 lb. bulk pork sausage	1/2 tsp. nutmeg
2 Tbsp. chopped onion	1/4 tsp. salt
6 Tbsp. all-purpose flour	worcestershire sauce
1 quart milk	hot pepper sauce
1/2 tsp. poultry seasoning	

Crumble sausage into a large saucepan. Cook over medium heat. Add onion and cook until transparent. Drain all but 2 tablespoons of drippings. Stir in flour. Cook over medium heat for about 6 minutes or mixture turns golden. Stir in milk. Add seasonings to taste. Cook, stirring until thickened. Serve with hot biscuits. Yield: 4 to 6 servings.

BAKED OATMEAL

1/2 c. butter, melted	3 c. quick oats
3/4 c. brown sugar	1 tsp. cinnamon
2 eggs, beaten	2 tsp. baking powder
1 tsp. salt	1 c. milk

Mix everything together and pour in a greased 8 in. square pan. Bake at 350° for 30 min. Serve with warm milk or fresh fruit.

CORN MEAL MUSH

Heat 2 c. water in a stir pan. Put 1 c. cornmeal, 1/4 c. flour and 1 teaspoon salt in a big kettle. Stir in 1 c. cold water. Boil for 20 min.

Ruby Beachy

FRIED CORNMEAL MUSH

3 c. yellow cornmeal
1 tsp. salt
2 qts. boiling water
1/2 c. white flour

    Mix together cornmeal, flour, and salt. Slowly add dry ingredients to boiling water, stirring constantly to prevent lumps. Cook until it leaves side of saucepan. Pour into flat pans to mold or use 1 bread pan. Set in refrigerator to chill thoroughly. Cut in slices 1/4 inch thick and fry until golden brown on both sides. Delicious with hot maple syrup or any kind of gravy.

BAKED STUFFED EGGS

8 hard cooked eggs
3 to 4 Tbsp. sour cream
SAUCE:
1/2 c. chopped onion
2 Tbsp. butter or oleo
10 3/4 oz. can cream of mushroom soup, undiluted
2 tsp. prepared mustard
1/2 tsp. salt

8 oz. sour cream
1/2 c. shredded cheddar cheese
1/2 tsp. paprika

    Slice eggs in half lengthwise. Remove yolks and set whites aside. In a bowl, mash yolks with a fork. Add sour cream, mustard and salt. Mix well. Fill the egg whites. Set aside. In a saucepan saute onions in butter until tender. Add soup and sour cream, mix well. Pour half into an ungreased 7 x 11 x 2" baking pan. Arrange stuffed eggs over the sauce. Spoon remaining sauce on top. Sprinkle with cheese and paprika. Cover and refrigerate overnite. Remove 1/2 hour before baking. Bake at 350° for 25 to 30 min., uncovered. Yield: 6 to 8 servings.

TACOED EGGS

8 eggs, beaten
1/2 c. shredded cheese
2 Tbsp. chopped onion
1/2 c. taco seasoned ground beef
2 Tbsp. chopped green pepper
1 - 4 drops hot pepper sauce
flour tortillas, warmed
salsa, optional

    In a bowl combine eggs, cheese, onion, green pepper, and pepper sauce. Cook and stir in a nonstick skillet until eggs begin to set. Add meat and cook until eggs are completely set. Spoon into a warm tortilla and roll up, top with salsa. Yield: 4 servings.

My Favorite Recipes:

My Favorite Recipes:

Breads, Rolls, and Pastries

MOM'S BREAD

3/4 c. lard
3/4 c. honey
3/4 qt. warm water
2 Tbsp. yeast
salt
flour

Mix yeast and water. Add 1/2 tablespoon sugar. After yeast is dissolved add lard and honey. For wheat bread add 1 to 2 cups wheat flour and let set 1/2 hour. Add sapphire flour, and work in. Knead until it's not sticky. Let rise until double. Punch down and repeat. Divide and put into greased loaf pans and let rise again. Bake at 350° for 1/2 hour.

Mrs. Miriam Troyer

WHITE BREAD

5 tsp. yeast
3/4 c. lukewarm water
3/4 c. white sugar
pinch of salt
1 Tbsp. vinegar
1 tsp. lard
2 3/4 pt. warm water

Dissolve yeast in 3/4 cup lukewarm water. Start this with about 14 cups white flour. Work in flour and knead until dough feels right. Quinch down every half hour. Let rise until double in size. Form in loaves and put in pans. Let set in warm place until ready to bake. Bake at 375° for 30 min. Yield: 10 - 1 lb. loaves.

Alma Hershberger

HOMEMADE BREAD

3 pkg. yeast
3 c. warm water
1/3 c. brown sugar
1/3 c. white sugar
1 1/2 Tbsp. salt
3 Tbsp. flour
3/4 c. vegetable oil
8 c. flour

Dissolve yeast in water. Mix sugar, salt and 3 Tbsp. flour. Add to yeast mixture. Stir, add oil, then gradually work in flour. Place in a lightly greased bowl. Cover and let rise 1/2 hour. Punch down then let rise another 1/2 hour. Work dough again, then let rise for 1 hour. Punch down and form into 5 or 6 loaves. Put in greased pans and let rise approximately 1 hour or until raised 1/2 inch above pan. Bake at 325° for 30 min.

Note: For brown bread use 3 c. wheat flour and 5 c. white.

WHOLE WHEAT BREAD

2 c. lukewarm water
1/2 c. milk
3 Tbsp. brown sugar, level
1 Tbsp. white sugar
1 c. shortening
1 pkg. yeast
2 tsp. salt
2 c. whole wheat flour
2 1/2 c. white flour

Dissolve yeast in warm water. Add all other ingredients except for wheat flour. Let stand and rise for 15 minutes. Work in whole wheat flour. Knead well and let rise 30 min. Punch down and let rise till double. Form into loaves and prick tops with fork. Let rise again until double and bake at 350° for 30 min.

Mrs. Ora Lena Miller

BROWN BREAD

In a large bowl put:
1 1/3 Tbsp. salt
1 lg. egg
1 1/3 Tbsp. brown sugar
1/3 c. baking molasses
1/3 c. melted shortening
2 3/4 c. warm water

Meanwhile dissolve 1 heaping teaspoon white sugar in 1/2 c. warm water. Add 2 tablespoons yeast to the water and sugar. Let rise to 1 c. Add to other mixed ingredients. Add 1 1/3 c. wheat flour and enough white flour to form a stiff dough. Let rise 15 min., knead down. Let rise 30 min. Knead down again. Let rise 1 hour; knead. Bake at 375° for 25 minutes. Yield: 4 loaves.

Mrs. Ada Mullet

MONKEY BREAD

1/4 c. scalded milk
1 tsp. salt
1/4 c. shortening
1/4 c. sugar
1 egg, beaten
1 pkg. dry yeast
1/4 c. lukewarm water
4 c. sifted flour

In a large bowl cool scalded milk to lukewarm. Add salt, sugar, egg, and shortening. Dissolve yeast in warm water and add to milk mixture. Add flour and beat well. Brush dough with oil. Place in a large greased bowl and cover with a towel. Let rise in warm place until double in size. Turn out on lightly floured board. Knead until smooth. Shape into 1" balls. Dip each in melted oleo or butter and then in granulated sugar. Drop onto a greased cookie sheet, making 2 or 3 layers. Bake at 400° for around 20 min.

Nora Yoder

2 HOUR DINNER ROLLS

3 pkgs. yeast
2 c. warm water
1/2 c. white sugar
2 eggs
4 Tbsp. shortening
1 tsp. salt
6 - 6 1/2 c. Thesco bread flour

Dissolve yeast in water. Add sugar and eggs then beat until foamy. Stir in shortening, salt and flour. Mix and knead just enough to blend well. Let rise until double. Form into buns and let rise again. Bake at 400° for 15 to 20 minutes. If all goes well these can be made in 2 hours.

Mrs. Nettie Miller

QUICK DINNER BUNS

1 1/2 c. milk
2 Tbsp. yeast
2 Tbsp. melted butter
1 tsp. salt
1 c. water
2 eggs
3/4 c. white sugar
7 c. Robin Hood flour

Scald milk and cool. Put yeast in water and let stand for 5 min. Beat eggs. Add sugar, salt and butter, then add cooled milk and yeast mixture. Add flour. Mix well. Let rise until double. Shape into buns and let rise again. Bake at 350° for 15 to 20 min.

Susie Yoder

DINNER ROLLS

3 c. milk, scalded
3/4 c. sugar
1/2 c. oleo
1 Tbsp. salt
2 eggs, beaten
2 pkg. yeast
3 c. donut mix
6 c. flour

Add sugar, oleo, salt and eggs to hot milk. Cool to lukewarm. Add yeast and let set 10 minutes. Then add donut mix and flour. Let rise once, work down and let rise again. Make buns and let rise. Bake at 350° for 20 min. Yield: 70 buns.

Elmina Beachy

~ Happiness isn't getting what you want; it's wanting what you have. ~

SWEET ROLLS

1 c. milk, scalded
1/2 c. oleo
1/3 c. sugar
1/2 tsp. salt
2 eggs
1 pkg. yeast
1/4 c. warm water

    Dissolve yeast in warm water. Melt oleo in hot milk. Mix altogether and refrigerate overnight.

Marie Kline

BUNS

1 c. lard
3/4 c. sugar
2 Tbsp. salt
1 c. boiling water
1/2 c. boiled milk
2 pkgs. yeast dissolved in 1 c. warm water
2 eggs
8 c. flour

Anna Yoder

SPOON BREAD

1 can creamed corn
1 can regular corn, drained
8 oz. sour cream
2 eggs, slightly beaten
1/2 c. margarine, softened
1 box jiffy muffin mix

    Mix together and bake at 350° for approximately 45 min. Delicious with any Mexican meal.

GOLDEN CORNBREAD

1 c. yellow cornmeal
1/4 c. sugar
1 c. sifted flour
1/2 tsp. salt
4 tsp. baking powder
1 c. milk
1 egg
1/4 c. shortening or oil

    Sift together dry ingredients in a bowl. Add egg, milk and shortening. Beat with egg beater or spoon for about 1 min. Do not over beat. Bake in a greased 8" square pan or muffin tins at 425° for 20 to 25 min.

Mrs. Margaret Yoder

MEXICAN CORNBREAD

2 c. cornmeal	1/4 c. pimentos
1 c. flour	2 1/2 c. sweet milk (milk)
2 tsp. baking powder	1/2 c. cooking oil
1 tsp. salt	3 eggs, beaten
1 1/2 c. grated cheese	1 large onion
1/2 c. or less hot peppers	2 tsp. white sugar
1/4 lb. bacon, fried crisp	1 c. cream style corn

Mix together. Bake at 400° for around 35 min. Delicious served with:

1 lb. hamburger	1 pkg. taco seasoning
1 can kidney beans	

Stir together and serve with cornbread.

Barb Byler

EASY FRENCH BREAD

Dissolve:

2 pkg. dry yeast	1/2 c. warm water
1/2 tsp. sugar	

Combine:

2 Tbsp. sugar	2 Tbsp. fat
2 tsp. salt	2 c. boiling water

Cool to lukewarm and add to yeast mixture. Stir in 7 1/2 to 8 c. flour. Knead 10 minutes or until smooth and elastic. Place in ungreased bowl turning once. Let rise until doubled. Punch down and let rise 15 min. Divide dough in half. On floured surface roll each half to a 12" by 15" rectangle. Roll up starting at 15" edge. Place loaves on greased cookie sheets and make 4 or 5 slashes diagonally across tops. Let rise until double. Mix and brush on: 1 egg, beaten with 2 Tbsp. milk. Sprinkle on poppy or sesame seeds if desired. Bake at 400° for 20 min.

TOASTY GARLIC BREAD

1 french bread (12 to 15") cut in 1" slices	Parmesan cheese parsley flakes
1/2 c. butter, softened	garlic powder

Spread both sides of bread with butter. Place cut side down, on a cookie sheet. Sprinkle one side with cheese, parsley and garlic powder. Broil 4" from heat until light golden brown. Turn slices and repeat with other side. Serve immediately. Yield: 12 to 15 slices.

DELICIOUS APPLE BREAD

1 c. sugar
1/2 c. shortening
1 tsp. vanilla
1 tsp. soda
2 Tbsp. buttermilk or sour milk
1 tsp. cinnamon
2 c. flour
2 c. chopped apples
2 Tbsp. sugar
1 egg

Mix soda with buttermilk or sour milk. Beat 1 c. sugar with shortening. Blend in soda mixture, egg, vanilla, flour and apples. Put batter in bread pan. Sprinkle sugar and cinnamon on top. Bake at 350° for 50 to 60 min.

BANANA NUT BREAD

1/2 c. shortening
1 c. sugar
2 eggs
3 bananas
2 c. flour
1/2 tsp. soda
1/2 tsp. baking powder
1/2 tsp. salt
1/2 c. nuts

Cream shortening, sugar, and eggs. Sift together dry ingredients. Add alternately with mashed bananas. Fold in nuts. Bake in a greased loaf pan at 350° for approximately 45 min.

ZUCCHINI BREAD

3 eggs
3 c. flour
1 tsp. soda
1 tsp. salt
2 tsp. vanilla
1 1/2 c. chopped walnuts
1 1/2 c. coconut
1 c. cooking oil
2 c. white sugar
1 tsp. cinnamon
1 tsp. baking powder
3 c. grated zucchini squash, do not peel

Beat together sugar and eggs until creamy. Add oil and vanilla. Mix well. Stir in all dry ingredients. Fold in zucchini, coconut, and nuts. Bake in greased and floured pans for 1 hour at 350°. Yield: 3 loaves.

Mrs. Ora Lena Miller

~ *Keeping house is like threading beads on a string with no knot at the end.* ~

OVERNIGHT CINNAMON ROLLS

2 eggs, beaten
1/3 c. white sugar
1/2 tsp. salt
1 pkg. yeast
1/4 c. warm water
1 c. milk, scalded
1/2 c. oleo
3 1/2 c. Robin Hood flour

Dissolve yeast in 1/4 c. warm water. Add rest of ingredients and refrigerate overnite. Roll out cold dough. Sprinkle with butter, cinnamon and a little brown sugar. Roll up and cut in slices. Put pecan topping in bottom of a greased pan, then put rolls on top of that. Let rise, then bake.

PECAN TOPPING FOR ROLLS:
1/3 c. butter
1/2 c. brown sugar
1/2 c. pecan pieces
1 Tbsp. corn syrup or water

When rolls are done baking flip out on plate.

Mary Anna Troyer

CREAM STICKS

2 pkgs. dry yeast soaked in 1 c. warm water
1 c. scalded milk
1/2 c. butter or oleo
2/3 c. sugar
2 eggs, well beaten
1 tsp. salt
6 c. flour

Put butter, sugar, eggs and salt into scalding milk. Let cool. Add yeast and flour and let rise once. Roll out and cut in strips. Fry in deep fat. Make a slit in side and fill with filling while still warm.

FILLING:
Mix and set aside.
2 1/3 c. powdered sugar
1 egg white, beaten
1/4 tsp. salt

Boil 1 minute:
2 Tbsp. water
1/2 c. white sugar

Add to first mixture. Then add 1 teaspoon vanilla and 1/2 c. Crisco.

~ Not one person in a thousand can keep his hands in his pockets while giving directions. ~

SIMPLE DOUGHNUTS

3 1/2 c. flour
2 Tbsp. oil
2 eggs, beaten
1 tsp. nutmeg or vanilla
1 c. white sugar
3/4 c. milk
5 Tbsp. baking powder

   Mix above ingredients on floured surface. Cut with doughnut cutter. Let rise for 15 min. Fry in deep hot fat at 375° until brown. Roll in sugar.

DOUGHNUTS

3/4 c. milk
1/4 c. sugar
1 tsp. salt
1/4 c. margarine
1/4 c. warm water
1 pkg. yeast
1 egg, beaten
3 1/4 c. flour

   Scald milk, stir in sugar, salt and margarine. Cool to lukewarm. Place water in a large bowl. Sprinkle in yeast, stir until dissolved. Add milk mixture, egg and half of the flour. Beat until smooth. Stir in enough additional flour to make a soft dough. Turn dough out onto a lightly floured board. Knead until smooth and elastic, about 10 min. Place in bowl. Cover and let rise until double in bulk. Punch down and roll out about 1/2" thick and cut with donut cutter. Place on floured sheet pans. Let rise until double in size. Fry in Wesson oil at 375°. Dip in Glaze.

GLAZE:
2 c. powdered sugar
1/3 c. milk
1 tsp. vanilla

BUTTER TARTS

1 c. brown sugar
1 egg
3 Tbsp. butter
2 Tbsp. corn syrup
1 tsp. vanilla
pastry for (9") crust

   Mix sugar and butter together. Add egg, syrup and vanilla. Combine well. Line 6 tart pans with pastry. Place 2 large spoonfuls of mixture in each. Bake at 400° for about 20 min. or until pastry is slightly browned.

FILLED BUTTER HORNS

Blend 4 c. of flour and 1 c. of butter. (Mix like pie crust.) Then combine the following ingredients:

4 egg yolks	**3 Tbsp. sugar**
2 pkgs. yeast	**1/2 pt. thick sour cream**
1/2 tsp. salt	

Add to flour mixture and mix together lightly like a pie crust. Form into little balls. Do not overwork dough. Place balls on a cookie sheet and cover with waxed paper and a towel to prevent drying. Let stand in a cool place overnight. Use a floured rolling pin to roll out each ball on a floured board, about 1/8" thick in a triangle shape. Spread with filling. Roll up and form horns. Bake at 300°. After 6 min. brush with beaten eggs (whole of yolks) to which a dash of cream has been added. Bake 20 min. longer.

FILLING:

Beat 4 egg whites till stiff. Fold in 1 c. sugar and 2 c. finely chopped nuts.

My Favorite Recipes:

My Favorite Recipes:

Main Dishes and Vegetables

SAUCE FOR MEATLOAF, CHICKEN, AND HAMBURGERS

1 1/2 - 2 c. catsup
6 Tbsp. brown sugar
1 tsp. mustard
1 tsp. vinegar
1 tsp. worcestershire sauce
pinch of salt

Mrs. Ida Miller

CHICKEN BARBEQUE SAUCE

1 qt. vinegar
11 tsp. salt
4 tsp. worcestershire sauce
1 lb. butter
1 qt. water
oregano flakes

Soak chicken overnite in sauce. Barbeque.

Mrs. Wilma Hochstetler

BBQ SAUCE

2 gallons water
1 1/2 gal. vinegar
5 lbs. butter
13 oz. salt
6 Tbsp. worcestershire sauce

Yield: enough for 75 halves of chicken.

Barbara Troyer

BBQ SAUCE FOR HAM

1 c. catsup
1 c. water
2 Tbsp. worcestershire sauce
1/4 c. vinegar
3 Tbsp. brown sugar

Heat and pour over sliced ham. Bake at 350° till done.

Mrs. Lizzie Keim

CONEY SAUCE

5 lbs. hamburger
1 1/4 stick oleo
5/8 c. flour
5 c. ketchup
2 1/2 c. BBQ sauce
1/3 c. mustard
a little brown sugar
1 lg. onion, chopped
1 green pepper, shredded

Brown oleo, add flour, then hamburger. Cook till done. Add rest of ingredients. Simmer for 1/2 hour.

Marie Kline

ELLA'S AWESOME CHICKEN

Chicken pieces, thighs, drumsticks, and etc.
Hickory smoke BBQ sauce (thick and spicy)

Remove skin from chicken pieces. Marinate overnite in BBQ sauce, enough to cover all pieces. Bake (still in sauce) around 1 hour at 350°, or until chicken is tender.

Barb Byler

OVEN BARBECUED CHICKEN

Fry chicken until brown. Place in a 9 x 13" pan.
SAUCE:

3 Tbsp. butter	3 Tbsp. brown sugar
1/3 c. onions	1/2 c. water
3/4 c. ketchup	2 tsp. mustard
1/3 c. vinegar	1 Tbsp. worcestershire sauce

Simmer for 15 min. Pour over chicken and bake uncovered for 1 hour at 350° basting occasionally.

Linda Miller

DELICIOUS BBQ CHICKEN

6 skinless chicken breasts	1/4 c. brown sugar
1 c. crunchy peanut butter	3/4 c. salsa
1/3 c. chopped cilantro	1 1/2 tsp. salt
1/2 c. kimlan soy sauce	1/4 tsp. cayenne pepper
1/4 c. lemon juice	3 Tbsp. minced onion
1/2 tsp. black pepper	

Combine all ingredients except chicken. Mix well. Add chicken. Marinate overnite or at least 4 hours. Bar-B-Q.

Ruth Ann Troyer

~ When life gives you lemons, make lemonade. ~

HUNGARIAN CHICKEN

6 Tbsp. all-purpose flour	1 to 2 Tbsp. paprika
salt and pepper	1 tsp. sugar
1 broiler-fryer chicken, cut up	1 tsp. salt
1/4 c. butter, divided	1 bay leaf
1 onion, chopped	2/3 c. chicken broth
2/3 c. tomato juice	2/3 c. sour cream

Combine flour, salt and pepper and place in a plastic bag. Shake chicken a few pieces at a time in flour mixture. Melt 1 tablespoon butter in a large skillet. Saute onion until tender. Remove from pan and set aside. In same skillet, melt remaining butter and brown chicken on both sides. Combine tomato juice, paprika, sugar, and salt. Pour over chicken. Add bay leaf, broth and reserved onion. Cover and simmer until tender, about 1 hour. Remove chicken to a platter and keep warm. Reduce heat to low, remove bay leaf and stir in sour cream. Heat 2 to 3 min. Do not boil. Pour desired amount over chicken. Serve immediately. Yield: 4 to 6 servings.

HONEY MUSTARD CHICKEN

1/2 c. salad dressing	1 Tbsp. honey
2 Tbsp. Dijon mustard	4 boneless, skinless chicken breast halves

Mix salad dressing, mustard and honey. Place chicken on greased grill over medium hot coals. Brush with 1/2 of the salad dressing mixture. Grill for 8 to 10 minutes. Turn and brush with remaining salad dressing mixture. Continue grilling until chicken is tender. Note: can also broil on broiler pan 5 to 7" from heat. Follow same instructions as for grilling.

POOR MAN'S STEAK

3 lbs. hamburger	salt and pepper
1 c. crushed crackers	chopped onion
1 c. water	worcestershire sauce

Mix all together. Add seasonings to taste. Spread on cookie sheet and chill overnite. Next morning cut in squares and brown. Place in a baking dish and pour 2 cans cream of mushroom soup and 1 can water over meat and bake for 2 hours at 325°.

Nora Yoder

POOR MAN'S STEAK

2 lbs. hamburger
1 c. cracker crumbs
salt and pepper
milk or water

Shape in roll and refrigerate overnite. Slice and fry. Pour 1 can cream of mushroom soup on top and bake 1 hour at 350°.

Karen Raber

BAR-B-Q STEAK

1 c. Regina's Red wine vinegar
1/4 c. worcestershire sauce
3 dashes pepper
1 tsp. salt
1/2 c. vegetable oil

Mix above and soak steaks 3 or more hours, 1 1/2 hour on each side.

Mary Anna Troyer

CHICKEN FRIED STEAK

1 lb. ground beef
1/2 c. flour
1 tsp. salt
1/4 tsp. pepper

Mix well. Shape into flat patties. Dip into a beaten egg and roll in cracker crumbs. Fry like hamburgers in a skillet. It takes approximately 7 min. to fry them.

Mrs. (Henry) Edna Miller

MOCK HAM LOAF

1 lb. hamburger
1/2 lb. Trail bologna, ground
1 c. cracker crumbs
1 egg
1 tsp. salt
1/2 of glaze (below)

Mix together and shape into a loaf. Baste with remaining glaze and bake at 350° for 1 to 1 1/2 hour.

GLAZE:
3/4 c. brown sugar
1/2 tsp. dry mustard
1 Tbsp. vinegar
1/2 c. water

Heat until sugar melts.

Mrs. Miriam Troyer

~ When looking for faults, use a mirror not a telescope. ~

HAM LOAF

5 lb. ham loaf mix 1/2 c. bread crumbs
6 eggs 1/2 c. milk
1 c. graham cracker crumbs

Mix together all ingredients. Form into a loaf and put in roaster pan. Bake at 350° for 2 1/2 hours.

TOPPING:
1/2 c. ketchup 1/4 c. brown sugar
1 Tbsp. mustard

Mix together and spread over ham loaf the last 1/2 hour of baking.

HAM LOAF

2 eggs 1 1/2 lbs. ground fully
1 c. milk cooked ham
1 c. dry bread crumbs 1/2 lb. ground pork
1/4 tsp. pepper

GLAZE:
1/3 c. packed brown sugar 1/2 tsp. dry mustard
1/4 c. vinegar 2 Tbsp. water

Beat eggs, add milk, bread crumbs, and pepper. Add ham and pork, mix well. In a shallow baking pan, shape meat mixture into a loaf, about 8 x 4 x 2 1/2". Insert a meat thermometer. Bake at 350° for 30 min. Meanwhile, combine glaze ingredients. Spoon over loaf, continue baking until thermometer reaches 170°. (About 40 minutes longer.) Baste occasionally with glaze. Yield: 8 servings.

MEAT LOAF

1 1/2 lbs. ground beef 1/2 tsp. pepper
3/4 c. cracker crumbs 1 egg
1/4 c. onion 3/4 c. milk
1 1/2 tsp. salt

Mix altogether and put in loaf pan. Bake at 350° for 40 min. Spread the following sauce on top and bake an additional 10 min.

SAUCE:
2/3 c. catsup 2 Tbsp. brown sugar
1 Tbsp. prepared mustard

MEATLOAF

18 lbs. hamburger
9 c. oatmeal
2 onions, chopped
18 tsp. salt
3 tsp. pepper
9 cups milk

Mrs. Ida Miller

MEAT BALLS IN GRAVY

2 lbs. ground beef
1/2 c. celery, diced
1/2 c. onion, chopped
2 eggs, beaten
1 1/2 tsp. salt
1/2 tsp. pepper

Mix all ingredients and shape into balls. Brown in margarine and arrange in baking dish. Heat 1 can cream of mushroom soup with 1 can milk and pour over meat balls. Bake at 350° for 45 min.

Diane Keim

BAR-B-Q MEAT BALLS

3 lbs. hamburger
12 oz. evaporated milk
1 c. oatmeal
1 c. cracker crumbs
2 eggs
1/2 c. chopped onions
1/2 tsp. garlic powder
2 tsp. salt
1/2 tsp. pepper
2 tsp. chili powder

SAUCE:
2 c. catsup
1 c. brown sugar
1 tsp. liquid smoke
1/2 tsp. garlic powder
1/4 c. chopped onion

Pour sauce over meatballs. Bake at 350° for 1 hour.

Mary Anna Troyer

~ Worry is like a rocking chair . . . It gives you something to do but gets you nowhere. ~

SAVORY MEATBALLS

2 eggs, lightly beaten
1 onion, chopped
2 tsp. dry mustard
1 tsp. salt
1/2 tsp. pepper
1/2 tsp. poultry seasoning
1/3 c. cornmeal

2 lbs. ground beef
3 Tbsp. shortening
2 cans(10 3/4 oz. ea.) cream of mushroom soup
1 1/2 c. water
3/4 c. milk

In a mixing bowl, combine eggs, onion, mustard, salt, pepper, poultry seasoning, cornmeal and milk. Add beef and mix well. Shape into 2" balls. In a skillet melt the shortening over medium-high heat. Brown meatballs. Place in a casserole dish. Combine soup and water, pour over meatballs. Bake uncovered at 350° for 45 to 50 min. Yield: about 8 servings.

BAR-B-Q HAMBURGERS

1/2 c. water
1/2 c. sugar
1/2 c. homemade catsup
3/4 tsp. salt

2 Tbsp. vinegar
2 Tbsp. mustard
1 Tbsp. flour
onions, chopped

Use approximately 1 to 1 1/2 lbs. of hamburger to form patties. Pour sauce over them and bake.

Anita Troyer

SIZZLE BURGERS

Heat 1 Tbsp. butter in skillet with 3 Tbsp. worcestershire sauce. (French's) Cook 4 hamburgers patties in skillet turning to brown both sides. Season with salt and pepper.

~ Learn from yesterday, live for today, hope for tomorrow. ~

GROUND BEEF GRANDSTYLE

1 can oven-ready biscuits	1/4 c. catsup
8 oz. cream cheese	1/4 c. milk
1/2 c. onion	1 1/4 lbs. ground beef
3/4 tsp. salt	1 can cream of mushroom or chicken soup

Brown hamburger, add onion. Drain. Add cream cheese, soup, milk, and catsup. Season to taste. Top with biscuits. Bake at 350° for 15 to 20 min. or until biscuits are golden brown.

Mrs. Naomi Yoder

SHIP WRECK

1 lb. hamburger	5 med. potatoes
1 med. onion	1 can mushroom soup

Brown hamburger and put it in a baking dish. Dice in a layer of onion and then potatoes. Pour soup on top and cover with milk. Bake at 350° for 1 1/2 hour.

PANSY SUPPER CASSEROLE

1 lb. weiners, cut up	2 cans peas or 1 qt. vegetables, drained
4 Tbsp. minced onion	salt & pepper
8 med. potatoes, diced & cooked	1 can cream of mushroom soup
1/2 c. butter, browned	Velveeta cheese

Mix and bake for 35 min. at 350°.

Mary Anna Troyer

YUM-A-SETTA

1 lb. hamburger	1 can cream of tomato soup
1 pkg. wide noodles	1 lb. velveeta cheese
1 can cream of chicken soup	salt to taste

Fry hamburger. Cook noodles in water until tender, but not too soft. Mix tomato soup with hamburger and chicken soup with noodles. Put in layers in a casserole dish. Top with velveeta cheese and bake in slow oven for 1 hour at 250° to 300°.

MEXICAN GOULASH

1 lb. ground beef	1 tsp. dried oregano
1 c. chopped onion	1 tsp. salt
1/2 c. chopped green pepper	1/2 c. long-grain rice, uncooked
1 garlic clove, minced	
1 c. tomato juice	1 c. frozen corn
8 oz. kidney beans, undrained	1/2 c. black olives, sliced
4 tsp. chili powder	1 c. shredded cheese

In large skillet, over medium heat, cook hamburger, onion, pepper, and garlic till meat is brown and vegetables are tender. Drain fat. Add tomato juice, kidney beans, chili powder, oregano, salt and rice. Cover and simmer for about 25 min. or until rice is tender. Stir in corn and olives, cook 5 more minutes. Sprinkle with cheese and cover only till cheese melts, around 5 min.

Barb Byler

EL-PASO CASSEROLE

1 3/4 lb. velveeta cheese	1 1/2 lb. noodles
2 lbs. ham	1/2 lb. butter
WHITE SAUCE:	
1 c. flour	1/2 gal. milk

Cook noodles in water. Drain. Blend cheese and ham in white sauce. Pour over noodles in oiled or greased pan. Sprinkle with bread crumbs. Pour melted butter over bread crumbs.

Elmina Beachy

MEXICAN CASSEROLE

1 lb. hamburger	1 bottle milk taco sauce
1/2 onion	chopped pepper
1 can mushroom soup	1 bag cheese doritoes
1 can chicken soup	1 pkg. grated cheese

Brown hamburger with onions. Mix in soup, sauce and pepper. Heat well. Layer in greased casserole dish, first doritoes then hamburger mixture. Repeat and top with cheese and doritoes. Bake at 350° for 20 min.

Clara Miller

SOUR CREAM NOODLE CASSEROLE

2 cans cream of chicken soup
6 oz. mushrooms
4 oz. noodles, cooked
cheese slices
1 lb. hamburger, browned
8 oz. sour cream
salt and pepper

Put half of noodles, hamburger, mushrooms, and cheese in layers. Mix the sour cream with the soup and pour over all. Top with more cheese. Bake at 350° until hot.

PARTY CASSEROLE

1 lb. ground beef
1/2 c. chopped onion
2/3 c. milk
8 oz. cream cheese
8 oz. wide noodles
1 1/2 c. whole kernel corn
1 can mushroom soup
1/4 c. pimento
1 1/2 tsp. salt
dash of pepper
crushed bread crumbs or potato chips

Brown hamburger, and onions. Drain, then add remaining ingredients with the exception of bread crumbs or chips. Place in a casserole dish, sprinkle with bread crumbs or chips. Bake at 350° for 30 min.

COMPANY CASSEROLE

2 lbs. ground beef
16 oz. tomato sauce
8 oz. cream cheese, softened
1 Tbsp. chopped green pepper
salt and pepper
3 Tbsp. butter
1 c. cottage cheese
1/4 c. sour cream
1/3 c. chopped onion
8 oz. pkg. noodles

Brown hamburger in one tablespoon butter. Remove from heat and stir in tomato sauce, salt and pepper. Combine onions and peppers with cheeses and sour cream. Cook noodles 7 to 8 min. in boiling salt water. Drain and rinse quickly in cold water. In a large well greased casserole dish spread half of noodles and cover with cheese mixture. Add remaining noodles and dot with remaining butter. Place meat mixture on top. Bake uncovered for 20 to 30 min. at 350°.

TACO CASSEROLE

1 c. crushed taco chips
1 lb. hamburger
15 oz. can tomato sauce
16 oz. pork and beans
1/2 pkg. taco seasoning
grated cheese

Grease a 9 x 13" pan. Put chips in bottom of pan. Brown hamburger and drain well. Add tomato sauce, pork and beans and taco seasoning. Pour over chips. Top with cheese. Bake at 350° for 30 min. Yield: serves 6.

CHICKEN AND BISCUIT CASSEROLE

8 slices bacon, fried & crumbled
2 1/2 c. chicken, cooked, cut up
1 pkg. frozen veg., cooked
1 can chicken soup
6 oz. shredded cheese
3/4 c. milk
1 1/2 c. Bisquick mix
2/3 c. milk
1 can french fried onions

Combine bacon, chicken and vegetables in a greased 8 x 12" baking dish. Mix together soup and 3/4 c. milk. Pour over chicken mixture. Bake uncovered, at 400° for 15 min. Combine Bisquick mix, 2/3 c. milk, and 1/2 can onions. Put on top of casserole. Bake, uncovered, 15 to 20 min. or until biscuits are brown. Top with remaining cheese and onions. Bake for 2 to 3 min., until onions are toasted.

RIGATONI

8 oz. rigatoni noodles, cooked
1 c. Hormel pepperoni, cubed
1/2 c. shredded parmesan cheese
1/2 c. diced onion
1/4 c. chopped fresh basil
2 cloves minced garlic
26 oz. spaghetti sauce
2 c. shredded mozzarella cheese

Heat oven to 375°. Layer half of the ingredients in the order listed, in a greased 9 x 13" pan. Repeat layers. Bake uncovered for 25 to 30 min. or until lightly browned. Yield: 6 servings.

~ If you wish another to keep a secret, first keep it yourself. ~

UNDERGROUND HAM CASSEROLE

8 c. ham, cooked & cubed	1/2 tsp. pepper
4 Tbsp. oleo	2 c. velveeta cheese
1/2 c. chopped onions	1/2 lb. browned bacon
1 Tbsp. worcestershire sauce	mashed potatoes with
2 cans mushroom soup	1 pint sour cream (no milk)

Place cubed ham, onions, pepper, mushroom soup, and worcestershire sauce in bottom of a casserole dish. Top with 1 c. velveeta cheese slices and put mashed potatoes over that. Top with remaining cheese. Put bacon on top of cheese and bake for 20 min. or until it bubbles up the sides.

Ruth Ann Miller

CHICKEN GUMBO

9 slices bread, cubed	1 c. milk
4 c. chicken, cooked & diced	1 c. chicken broth
1/4 c. butter	1 tsp. salt
4 eggs, well beaten	9 slices velveeta cheese
1/2 c. mayonnaise	2 cans cream of celery soup

Take off crusts of bread and set aside. Mix together butter, milk, mayonnaise, chicken broth, eggs and salt. Add undiluted soup. Place bread in bottom of dish. Layer chicken over bread. Next, layer soup mixture over chicken. Cover with cheese. Brown bread crusts with 1/4 c. melted butter; place on top. Bake 1 1/4 hours at 350°, uncovered.

TURKEY CASSEROLE

16 oz. bag wide noodles	1 can mushroom soup
2 c. turkey, cook & diced	1/2 c. milk
2 oz. chopped pimento	1 c. water
2 1/2 c. peas and carrots	2 c. shredded cheese

Cook noodles for 20 min. Drain. Combine soup, milk, water and cheese in medium saucepan. Heat to boiling, stirring frequently. Combine noodles, turkey, pimento, peas and carrots. Pour cheese sauce over noodles and mix. Place noodles in a 9 x 13" baking dish. Bake at 350° for 30 min. Yield: 8 servings.

TATOR TOT CASSEROLE

1 to 2 lbs. hamburger
1 onion, chopped
velveeta cheese
1 can cream of mushroom soup
1 1/2 c. milk
tator tots

Brown hamburger with onion. Drain. Put in a large casserole dish. Put velveeta cheese on top of hamburger. Add the milk to soup and pour over cheese. Cover with tator tots. Bake at 375° for 45 minutes.

SAUSAGE CASSEROLE

Cook 6 quart potatoes french fry style with salt, not too soft or they'll get mushy. Add 1 lg. container sour cream, velveeta cheese, 1 diced onion, pepper and 1 qt. smoked sausage. Bake at 350°.

Mrs. Laura Miller

MACARONI AND CHICKEN CASSEROLE

2 c. milk
2 c. uncooked macaroni
2 c. dried chicken
2 cans mushroom soup
diced onion
salt
pepper
onion powder
velveeta cheese

Put in a casserole dish and refrigerate overnite. Take out 1 hour before baking. Bake at 350° for 1 hour.

Laura Miller

DRIED BEEF CASSEROLE

1 c. milk
1 can cream of mushroom soup
1 c. shredded cheddar cheese
3 Tbsp. chopped onion
1 c. uncooked macaroni
1/4 lb. dried beef, cut up

Mix all ingredients together. Put in refrigerater for 3 hours or overnite. Bake at 350° for 1 hour.

Marie Troyer

PIZZA CASSEROLE

2 c. macaroni, cooked
2 lbs. hamburger
1 small onion
1 pt. pizza sauce
1 can mushroom soup
2 c. mozzarella cheese, shredded

Cook macaroni, brown hamburger and onion. Add sauce and soup. Mix well. Put in casserole dish, top with cheese. Bake at 350° for 30 min.

Diane Keim

PIZZA CASSEROLE

1 - 2 lbs. hamburger
1/2 green pepper
1 can mushroom soup
1 pt. pizza sauce
1 can mushrooms, undrained
1/4 tsp. garlic powder
1/4 tsp. oregano
1/4 c. parmesan cheese
8 oz. wide noodles or 1 lb. spaghetti

Brown hamburger. Add salt, pepper and onion to taste. Cook noodles 3 to 5 min.; drain. Place in bottom of baking dish. Add hamburger mixture and remaining ingredients. Top with mozzarella cheese and pepperoni. Bake at 350° for 1/2 hour.

Ruby Beachy, Mrs. Miriam Troyer

PIZZA CASSEROLE

1/2 c. butter
2 Tbsp. flour
2 c. milk
1/4 lb. velveeta cheese
1 lb. noodles
2 lbs. ground beef
4 c. spaghetti sauce

Melt butter in medium saucepan. Blend in flour until smooth. Add 2 c. milk and cook until thickened. Remove from heat and blend in velveeta cheese until smooth. Add cooked and drained noodles, ground beef also browned and drained, and spaghetti sauce. Put mixture in baking dish and top with pepperoni slices. Bake at 350° for 30 to 45 min. Remove from oven and top with shredded cheese. Return to oven until cheese is melted.

Mary Beth Troyer

SARAH'S CHICKEN DRESSING
1 c. chicken, cooked & cubed 1 potato, cubed & cooked
3/4 c. chicken broth 1 egg
1 c. celery, chopped parsley, optional
1 c. milk 1 Tbsp. flour
4 c. toasted bread crumbs salt and pepper

Mix flour and add milk a little at a time. Add egg, salt and pepper to taste. Add remaining ingredients. Let sit a few min. Fry in margarine or butter.

Sarah Yoder

CHICKEN AND RICE
1 c. uncooked rice 1 1/4 c. water
1 can cream of celery soup 1 pkg. dry onion soup mix
1 can cream of chicken soup boneless chicken pieces

Mix dry rice, soups and water in a flat dish or loaf pan. Add chicken pieces and sprinkle with soup mix. Cover tightly and bake at 350° for 2 hours. Do not remove lid while baking.

JR.'S FAVORITE
1 lb. hamburger 1 can mushroom soup
5 to 6 potatoes cheese

Mix hamburger as you would for meat loaf. Bake for 1/2 hour. Pour cream of mushroom soup on top of hamburger. Cook, peel and mash potatoes. Add milk, butter, and salt to make mashed potatoes and put on top of hamburger mixture. Top with cheese. Bake for another 1/2 to 1 hour.

Mrs. Sue Miller

BEEF AND MACARONI
1 lb. ground beef 30 oz. jar spaghetti sauce
1/2 c. salad dressing 7 oz. cooked macaroni

Brown hamburger, add salad dressing and spaghetti sauce. Pour over cooked and drained macaroni. Top with shredded cheese.

~ He who makes himself a bigshot - is often the first to be fired. ~

MACARONI WITH BEEF AND BEANS

1 lb. ground beef
1/3 c. chopped onion
16 oz. diced tomatoes with liquid
15 oz. undrained pinto beans
2 1/2 tsp. chili powder
1 tsp. salt
3/4 c. elbow macaroni, uncooked

In a large skillet brown beef and onion. Drain fat. Add remaining ingredients. Cover and simmer for about 20 min., stirring occasionally, till macaroni is tender. Thin with water if necessary. Yield: 4 to 6 servings.

Mrs. Joan Mast

CROCKPOT SUPPER

sliced potatoes
sliced carrots
frozen corn
sliced onions
chopped celery

Layer in crockpot in order given. Brown 1 to 1 1/2 pounds hamburger and add 10 oz. tomato soup and 1/2 c. water. Put in crockpot. Cook on low for 8 - 10 hours.

Mrs. Lizzie Keim

CHEESEBURGER PIE

1 lb. ground beef
1/2 c. chopped onion
1/2 tsp. salt
1/4 tsp. pepper
1 c. cheddar cheese
1 1/2 c. milk
3 eggs
3/4 c. buttermilk biscuit mix

Brown hamburger with onions, salt, and pepper. Spread in the bottom of a greased pie plate. Top with cheese. In a blender mix milk, eggs and biscuit mix. Pour over cheese. Bake uncovered at 400° for 30 min. or until knife inserted in the center comes out clean. Let stand for 5 min. before cutting. Yield: 4 to 6 servings.

Anita Troyer

~ *If you want your dreams to come true, don't oversleep.* ~

CRESCENT CHEESEBURGER PIE

1 lb. ground beef	1/4 tsp. dried oregano, crushed
1/2 c. chopped onion	
8 oz. tomato sauce	2 pkg. crescent rolls
4 oz. mushrooms, drained	3 eggs, separated
1/4 c. chopped parsley	6 slices American cheese
1/4 tsp. salt	1 Tbsp. water

Brown hamburger and onion. Drain. Stir in tomato sauce, mushrooms, parsley, salt, oregano and pepper. Set aside. Unroll 1 pkg. of rolls and separate dough into triangles. In lightly greased 9" pie plate arrange dough to form a pie shell, pressing edes together. Beat 3 egg whites together plus yolks from 2 eggs. Pour half of beaten eggs over pie shell. Spoon meat mixture into shell. Put cheese on top. Spread with remaining beaten eggs. Mix reserved egg yolk with water and set aside. Use second package of rolls to form a 12" square by pressing dough together and rolling it out. Brush edges of bottom crust with egg and water mixture. Place dough on top of filling. Trim, seal and flute edges. Cut slits in top crust. Brush with remaining egg and water mixture. Cover edge loosely with foil strip to prevent over browning. Bake at 350° for 20 min. Cover center of pie loosely with foil and bake 20 min. longer. Yield: 6 servings.

QUICK CHEESEBURGER BAKE

1 lb. ground beef	1/4 c. milk
3/4 c. onions, chopped	2 c. bisquick baking mix
10 3/4 oz. cheddar cheese soup	3/4 c. water
1 c. frozen mixed vegetables	1 c. shredded cheddar cheese

Heat oven to 400°. Generously grease a 9 x 13 x 2" baking dish. Cook hamburger and onion in skillet until hamburger is done. Drain. Stir in soup, vegetables, and milk. Then stir baking mix and water in baking dish until moistened; spread evenly. Spread hamburger mixture over batter. Sprinkle with cheese. Bake for 30 min. Yield: 8 to 10 servings.

~ *Any fault recognized, is half corrected.* ~

TACO PIE

1 can crescent rolls
1 lb. ground beef
2 - 8 oz. cans tomato sauce
1 pkg. taco seasoning
1/2 lb. shredded cheese
1 c. shredded lettuce
1/2 c. chopped tomatoes
sour cream

Press dough onto a 12" pizza pan. Prick with fork and bake 10 to 12 min. Top with meat combined with tomato sauce and taco seasoning. Sprinkle cheese on top and return to oven until cheese melts. Top with remaining ingredients.

SALMON LOAF

1 lb. salmon, drained & flaked
1 1/2 c. mashed potatoes
1 1/2 c. cracker crumbs
3/4 tsp. salt
3 Tbsp. lemon juice
2 Tbsp. butter, melted
2 Tbsp. chopped onion
2 eggs, beaten
1 1/2 c. milk
dash of pepper

Mix lightly, put in a 8 x 12" buttered baking dish. Bake at 350° for 50 min.

Mrs. (Junior) Edna Miller

BALLARD BISCUITS

1 lb. hamburger
1/2 c. chopped onions
1 can mushroom soup
1 can chicken soup
8 oz. cream cheese
1/4 c. milk
1/4 c. catsup
salt

Fry hamburger, onions and salt together until done. Add soup, cream cheese, milk and catsup. Put in a loaf pan and bake until bubbly. Remove from oven and put biscuits on top. Bake at 375° for 15 to 20 min. Make biscuits from bisquick or pancake mix.

Alma Hershberger

CHICKEN ENCHILADA

2 1/2 lb. chicken, cut up
1 small can green chili
1 can cream of chicken soup
1 c. sour cream
2-3 c. Monterey Jack cheese
salsa sauce

Mix together and roll into tortilla. Sprinkle with more cheese and salsa sauce. Bake at 350° for around 1/2 hour.

Barb Byler

HAYSTACK

2 c. cracker crumbs
2 c. boiled rice
2 lbs. browned hamburger
1 can cheddar cheese soup, diluted with 1 can milk(hot)
diced tomatoes
chopped lettuce
chopped onions
kidney or refried beans
shredded cheese
sour cream
taco sauce

Put all ingredients in separate bowls and make a hay stack in order given.

PORK CHOPS WITH SCALLOPED POTATOES

3 Tbsp. butter or oleo
3 Tbsp. all-purpose flour
1 1/2 tsp. salt
1/4 tsp. pepper
14 1/2 oz. chicken broth
6 rib or loin pork chops
2 Tbsp. cooking oil
6 c. thin sliced peeled potatoes
1 med. onion, sliced
paprika & chopped parsley
additional salt and pepper, optional

In a saucepan, melt butter and stir in flour, salt and pepper. Add chicken broth. Cook and stir constantly until mixture boils. Cook for 1 min. Remove from heat and set aside. In a skillet brown pork chops in oil. Season to taste with salt and pepper. In a greased 9 x 13" baking dish, layer potatoes and onion. Pour broth mixture over potatoes. Place pork chops on top. Cover and bake at 350° for 1 hr.; uncover and bake 30 min. longer or until potatoes are tender. If desired sprinkle with parsley & paprika. Yield: 6 servings.

TOSTADOS

2 lbs. hamburger
1 small onion, diced
taco seasoning
1 can Brooks hot chili beans
1 1/2 c. tomato juice

Fry hamburger with onions. Drain and add taco seasoning to taste. Add beans and tomato juice until right consistency. Heat. Layer the following ingredients in order given using hamburger mixture. Crushed doritoes, hamburger mixture, shredded cheese, shredded lettuce, sour cream, chopped tomatoes and hot or mild taco sauce.

Mrs. (Henry) Edna Miller

BEEF AND CHEESE ENCHILADAS

1 1/2 c. mozzarella cheese, divided
1 1/2 c. cheddar cheese, divided
3 oz. cream cheese, softened
1 c. picante sauce, divided
1 pepper, diced
1/2 c. onion, diced
3/4 lb. hamburger, browned
10 flour tortillas (7")
lettuce, tomatoes, & sour cream

Combine 1 c. mozzarella cheese, 1 c. cheddar cheese, and cream cheese with hamburger. Add 1/4 c. picante sauce, peppers, and onions. Mix well. Spoon approximately 1/4 c. cheese mixture down the center of each tortilla. Roll and place seam side down in a 9 x 13 x 2" baking dish. Spoon remaining picante sauce evenly over enchiladas. Cover with remaining cheeses. Bake at 350° for 20 min. or until hot. Serve with tomatoes, lettuce and sour cream.

Marie Troyer

$25,000 MEXICAN DISH

2 c. bisquick biscuit mix
1 c. water
2 (15 oz.) cans refried beans
2 lbs. hamburger
16 oz. salsa
3 c. shredded cheddar
16 oz. sour cream
chopped lettuce & tomato

Fry hamburger and season. Mix biscuit mix, water and beans. Spread in a greased 9 x 13" pan. Sprinkle fried hamburger on top. Spread salsa and cheese over hamburger. Bake at 350° for 30 min. Top with sour cream, lettuce, and tomatoes just before serving. Delicious!

Ruby Beachy

STROMBOLI

2 loaves frozen bread
Italian seasoning
1/2 lb. hamburger, browned
1/2 lb. baked ham
1/2 lb. bacon, fried
1/2 lb. pepperoni
shredded cheddar and monterey jack cheese

Let bread thaw and rise. Place on cookie sheet. Push out to corners. Layer chopped meats and cheese down the center and sprinkle seasoning on top. Roll up and pinch center and edges together. Bake at 350° for 30 to 35 min.

LASAGNA

1 pkg. wide lasagna noodles
1 jar spaghetti sauce
1/2 lb. mozzarella cheese
2 lbs. hamburger

Brown hamburger and cook noodles. Arrange noodles in a 9 x 13" pan alternating with layers of meat, sauce and cheese. Bake at 350° for 30 min.

Karen Raber

LASAGNA

hamburger, cooked
lasagna noodles, cooked
spaghetti sauce
mozzarella cheese
cottage cheese

In a large flat baking dish put a thin layer of meat and sauce. Place noodles on top of meat mixture and cheeses on top of that. Continue to layer until everything is used, beginning and ending with sauce; top with cheese. Bake at 375° for 45 min. Let stand 10 min. before serving.

Nora Yoder

CRESCENT ROLL LASAGNA

2 cans crescent rolls
1 Tbsp. milk
2 slices cheese

MEAT FILLING:
1 lb. hamburger
3/4 c. chopped onion
1/2 tsp. oregano
1 Tbsp. parsley flakes
1/2 tsp. basil leaves
6 oz. can tomato paste
dash of pepper

CHEESE FILLING:
1 c. dry cottage cheese
1 egg
3/4 c. grated cheese

Meat filling: Brown hamburger. Add remaining ingredients and simmer. **Cheese filling:** Combine all ingredients. **Crust:** Unroll 1 can crescent rolls. Put in bottom of pan. Put hamburger mixture on crust. Put cheese mixture on top of that, then put rest of hamburger on. Put mozzarella cheese on top. Put other crust on top. Spread with milk to make it golden brown. Bake at 350° for 20 to 30 min., or until crust is golden brown.

IRISH ITALIAN SPAGHETTI

1 lb. ground beef
1 onion, chopped
1 tsp. salt
1/4 Tbsp. pepper
2 Tbsp. salad oil
1 can mushroom soup

1 can tomato soup
1/2 Tbsp. chili powder
1/2 Tbsp. tabasco sauce
1/2 c. grated cheese
8 oz. spaghetti

Brown meat and onion in skillet with salad oil, salt and pepper. Simmer 10 min. Add soups, seasonings and cheese. Cover and simmer for 45 min. Cook spaghetti and drain. Serve with sauce.

GYPSY SPAGHETTI

1/2 lb. salami, cut in strips
4 c. tomato juice
4 oz. can tomato paste
4 oz. can mushrooms

1 tsp. sugar
1/2 tsp. oregano
1/4 tsp. basil
red pepper, chopped

Boil all ingredients together for 1 hour or until thick. Pour over 8 oz. hot, cooked spaghetti. Top with parmesan cheese.

Sarah Yoder

PORK CHOP SPAGHETTI

1 Tbsp. butter
6 pork chops
1/4 c. onion, chopped
15 oz. tomato sauce
1 1/2 oz. spaghetti sauce mix

3/4 to 1 c. water
1/2 c. grated
    parmesan cheese
8 oz. long spaghetti
1 c. shredded cheese

Melt butter in a skillet. Add pork chops and brown on both sides. Remove from skillet and saute onion until tender. Add tomato sauce, spaghetti sauce mix and water. Mix well. Reduce heat to low. Return chops to skillet. Cover and simmer 45 to 55 min. or until tender. If sauce is too thick add more water. Stir in parmesan cheese. Meanwhile, prepare spaghetti according to package directions. Drain and arrange spaghetti and chops on a serving platter. Spoon sauce over all. Sprinkle shredded cheese over pork chops. Yield: 6 servings.

~ If you listen while you teach, you usually learn a lot. ~

ONE SKILLET SPAGHETTI

1 lb. ground beef
2 medium onions, chopped
28 oz. tomatoes, diced & liquid reserved
3/4 c. chopped green peppers
1/2 c. water
2 tsp. salt
1 tsp. chili powder
8 oz. spaghetti, broken
1 c. shreddeed cheddar cheese

In skillet brown meat and onions over high heat. Drain. Stir in tomatoes with liquid, and all remaining ingredients except cheese. Heat the mixture to boiling, cover and reduce heat. Simmer, stirring frequently until spaghetti is tender, about 30 min. If necessary add additional water during cooking. Sprinkle with cheese. Cover and heat only till cheese is melted. Yield: 6 servings.

Mrs. Joan Mast

SPAGHETTI SUPREME

1 lb. hamburger
1 onion, chopped
salt
1/2 lb. spaghetti, cooked & drained
1/2 c. carrots, chopped & cooked
1/2 c. celery, chopped & cooked
1 can mushroom soup
1 can tomato soup
1 soup can tomato juice

Fry hamburger with onions and salt. Put in layers and bake at 350° for 1 1/2 hours. Before serving top with velveeta cheese and bake for another 10 to 15 min.

Mrs. Margaret Yoder

PIZZA CUPS

3/4 lb. ground beef
6 oz. tomato paste
1 Tbsp. instant minced onion
1 tsp. Italian seasoning
1/2 tsp. salt
10 oz. refrigerated biscuits
3/4 c. mozzarella cheese

Brown and drain hamburger. Stir in tomato paste, onion and seasonings. (Mixture will be thick.) Cook over low heat for 5 min., stirring frequently. Place biscuits in a greased muffin tin, press to cover bottom and sides. Spoon about 1/4 c. of meat mixture into cups and sprinkle with cheese. Bake at 400° for 12 min. or until golden brown. Yield: 12 pizza cups.

PIZZA DOUGH

1 Tbsp. dry yeast
1 c. warm water
3 c. flour
1 tsp. sugar
1 1/2 tsp. salt
1/4 c. salad oil

Dissolve yeast in warm water. Add sugar, salt, oil, and 1/2 of flour. Beat well. Add remaining flour and knead for 5 min.

Anita Troyer

PIZZA CRUST

1 c. warm water
1 Tbsp. yeast
2 Tbsp. sugar
2 Tbsp. vegetable oil
2 1/2 c. flour
1 tsp. salt

Dissolve yeast in warm water. Add other ingredients and let sit for 5 min. Press into a lightly greased pizza pan. Add your favorite pizza toppings and bake at 375° for 25 to 30 min. Yield: 1 crust.

JIFFY PIZZA DOUGH

2 c. flour
1 Tbsp. baking powder
1 tsp. salt
2/3 c. milk
1/3 c. salad oil

Put everything in a bowl; then mix. Press on pizza pan and bake at 350° for 15 to 20 min.

PIZZA BURGERS

2 lbs. hamburger
1 lb. bologna
1 lb. cheese
1 pint spaghetti sauce
1 Tbsp. sweet basil
1 tsp. salt
1/4 tsp. pepper
1 Tbsp. oregano

Brown hamburger and drain, then put in broiler pan and cool. Grind bologna and cheese and add to hamburger. Add rest of ingredients. Bake or broil. Spread on buns.

Nancy Miller

~ *A lie is like a snowball; the longer it rolls, the larger it gets.* ~

GERMAN PIZZA

1 lb. ground beef	2 Tbsp. butter
1/2 onion, chopped	6 med. potatoes
1/2 green pepper, diced	3 eggs, beaten
1 1/2 tsp. salt, divided	1/3 c. milk
1/2 tsp. pepper	2 c. shredded cheese

In a 12" skillet, over medium heat, brown beef with onions, green pepper, 1/2 tsp. salt and pepper. Remove from skillet and drain fat. Reduce heat to low and melt butter. Spread peeled and finely shredded potatoes over butter and sprinkle with remaining salt. Top with beef mixture. Combine eggs and milk, pour over beef mixture. Cook covered until potatoes are tender, about 30 min. Top with cheese and cover till cheese melts. Cut in squares to serve.

Mrs. Joan Mast

UPSIDE DOWN PIZZA

2 lbs. hamburger	pepperoni
salt and pepper	2 Tbsp. green peppers
1 Tbsp. chopped onion	grated cheese
2 c. pizza sauce	16 oz. sour cream
1 can mushrooms	1 can crescents

Brown hamburger and onions. Add salt, pepper and pizza sauce. Add mushrooms and pepperoni. Bake at 350° for 25 min. Remove and add sour cream and cheese. Unroll crescents and lay on top. Bake until crescents are brown.

SLOPPY JOES

1 lb. ground beef	2 tsp. worcestershire sauce
11 1/8 oz. can Italian tomato soup (Campbell's)	1/8 tsp. pepper
	1/4 c. water

Brown ground beef. Drain off fat. Add soup. water, pepper, and worcestershire sauce. Heat, stirring often. Serve on slightly toasted buns. Yield: 6 servings.

~ *Just remember, when you're over the hill, you begin to pick up speed.* ~

SLOPPY JOES

1 lb. ground beef
15 oz. can tomato sauce
1 c. chopped onion
1/4 c. ketchup
3 Tbsp. steak sauce
1/2 tsp. garlic salt
1/2 c. shredded
   cheddar cheese

Brown and drain hamburger. Stir in rest of ingredients except for cheese. Simmer uncovered, for 15 min. Sprinkle with cheese.

CHEESE HASHBROWNS

2 lbs. hashbrowns
1 can cream of chicken soup
2 c. cheddar cheese
1 onion, chopped
2 c. sour cream
1/2 c. oleo, melted
cornflakes, crushed

Mix altogether except for cornflakes. Put cornflakes on top mixed with melted oleo. Bake at 350° for 1 hour.

                                        Mrs. Lizzie Keim

PAPRIKA POTATOES

1/2 c. butter or oleo
1/4 c. all-purpose flour
1/4 c. grated parmesan cheese
pinch of garlic or onion salt
1 Tbsp. paprika
3/4 tsp. salt
1/8 tsp. pepper
6 med. potatoes

Peel and quarter potatoes lengthwise. Melt butter in a 9 x 13 x 2" baking pan. Combine remaining ingredients in large plastic bag; set aside. Rinse potatoes and drain well. Place half of potatoes in bag and shake well to coat. Place in single layer in baking pan. Repeat with remaining potatoes. Bake uncovered at 350° for 50 to 60 min. Turn once after 30 min. Yield: 4 to 6 servings.

                                        Mrs. Anna Troyer

SWEET POTATOES

2 c. brown sugar
1 c. water
1/4 c. flour
butter

Mix sugar and flour. Add water and butter. Boil until mixture thickens like honey. Pour over cooked and sliced sweet potatoes. Bake at 350° for 20 to 30 min.

                                        Mrs. Margaret Yoder

EASY SCALLOPED POTATOES

5 lbs. raw potatoes
1 onion, diced
salt
garlic salt
pepper
parsley flakes
1 stick butter
2 cans cream of mushroom soup

Peel and slice or shred potatoes. Place in a casserole dish in layers in order given. Season to taste. Dot each layer with butter. Last, add 3 1/2 to 4 c. milk. Cover and bake at 350° for 1 to 1 1/2 hrs.

Mrs. Miriam Troyer

SCALLOPED POTATOES

1 can chicken soup
1 can mushroom soup
2 cans milk
velveeta cheese
salt and pepper
10 potatoes, peeled and sliced thin
1 1/2 c. sour cream

Mix everything except velveeta cheese. Bake at 325° for about 2 hours or until potatoes are tender. Cut in velveeta cheese and stir into potatoes. Be sure to grease baking dish.

POTLUCK POTATOES

2 lbs. potatoes
1 tsp. salt
1/4 tsp. pepper
1/2 c. butter, melted
2 c. cornflakes, crushed
1/2 c. chopped onion
1 can cream of chicken soup
1 pint sour cream
2 c. velveeta cheese

Cook potatoes and put through ricer. Add all other ingredients except for cornflakes. Put into a greased 5 qt. casserole dish. Cover wiht crushed cornflakes mixed with 1/4 c. melted butter. Bake at 350° for 45 min.

Mrs. Esta Miller

~ A good angle to approach any problem
is the TRY-angle. ~

POTLUCK POTATOES

2 lbs. potatoes	1/4 tsp. pepper
1/2 c. butter	1 pint sour cream
1 can cream of mushroom soup	2 c. velveeta cheese
1 can cream of chicken or celery soup	1 tsp. lawry's salt
	1/2 c. melted butter
1 tsp. onion salt	
chopped onion, optional	

Slice potatoes and cook until almost tender. Mix the rest of ingredients together and heat until cheese is melted. Put in layers in casserole dish and cover with 2 c. crushed cornflakes mixed with 1/2 c. melted butter. Bake at 350° for 45 min.

Mrs. Ida Miller, Mrs. Miriam Troyer

POTLUCK POTATOES

2 lbs. frozen hash browns	1/2 c. milk
8 oz. french onion dip	1/2 c. chopped onion
1/2 c. butter, melted	1/4 tsp. pepper
8 to 10 oz. velveeta cheese	2 c. cornflakes or club crackers, crushed
1 can cream of chicken soup	

Mix together all ingredients except for cornflakes. Melt 1/4 c. butter and mix with cornflakes or crackers and sprinkle on top. Bake at 350° for 45 min.

Mrs. Mary Ann Hershberger

SPINACH MASHED POTATOES

6 to 8 lg. potatoes	1/4 tsp. pepper
3/4 c. sour cream	2 Tbsp. chopped chives
1 tsp. sugar	1/4 tsp. dill leaves
1/4 lb. butter	1 pkg. frozen spinach, chopped, cooked & well drained
2 tsp. salt	
1 c. shredded cheddar cheese	

Cook and mash potatoes. Add sour cream, sugar, butter, salt, and pepper. Beat until light and fluffy. Add chives, dill and spinach. Place in a casserole dish and sprinkle with cheese. Bake at 400° for 20 min. This can be made a day ahead and then baked just before serving.

EASY MASHED POTATOES

3 lbs. hot mashed potatoes
1/2 c. milk
1/4 c. butter
8 oz. cream cheese
2 eggs, beaten
1/4 c. onion, finely chopped
1/2 c. sour cream

Mash potatoes in large bowl. Cut cream cheese in small pieces and add to potatoes along with butter. Beat well until melted. Add sour cream. Mix eggs and milk. Add to mixture along with onions and salt. Beat well. Pour into a greased casserole dish and refrigerate overnight. Bake at 350° for 45 min. Serves 10 to 12 people.

Barbara Jean Mullet

GRILLED POTATOES

1/2 c. salad dressing
3 garlic cloves, minced
1/2 tsp. paprika
1/4 tsp. ea. salt & pepper
1 onion, sliced
3 potatoes, cut in 1/4" slices

Mix salad dressing and seasoning in a large bowl until well blended. Stir in potatoes and onions to coat. Divide potato mixture evenly among 6 - 12" squares of aluminum foil. Seal each to form a packet. Place on grill over medium hot coals. Grill, covered, 25 to 30 min. or until potatoes are tender. Yield: 6 servings.

POTATO PUFFS

2 eggs
1 c. mashed potatoes
1/2 c. all-purpose flour
1 1/2 tsp. baking powder
1/4 tsp. salt
oil for deep fat frying

Beat eggs. Add potatoes. Combine flour, baking powder, and salt. Stir into potato mixture. In a large saucepan or kettle, heat about 1" of oil to 375°. Drop mixture by heaping teaspoonsful into hot oil, 4 or 5 at a time. Fry 2 to 3 min. or until golden brown, turning once. Drain on paper towels. Serve immediately. Yield: 1 1/2 to 2 doz.

~ *Happiness can be thought, taught and caught - but not bought.* ~

RICE CASSEROLE

1 lb. hamburger, browned with chopped onion
3 1/2 c. water, part can be broth
1 c. uncooked rice
1 can cream of mushroom or chicken soup
3/4 c. chopped celery, optional
1 Tbsp. butter, melted
1 pkg. peas or mixed veg.
salt and pepper
1 tsp. worcestershire or soy sauce

Mix all together and pour into greased 2 or 3 quart casserole dish. Cover and bake at 375° for 1 hour, or at 350° for 1 1/4 hrs. Tator tots on top are also good.

Mrs. Miriam Troyer

CALIFORNIA RICE

1 c. raw rice
1 c. onion, chopped
1 lb. bulk sausage
1 can mushroom soup
1 c. celery, chopped
1 c. chicken, cooked & diced
salt and pepper
1 can water

Brown sausage, onion, celery, and chicken. Add soup, water from chicken and seasonings. Put in greased casserole dish. Bake for 2 hours at 325°.

Mrs. Anna Troyer

CHEESY RICE PATTIES

3 c. cooked brown rice
1/2 c. shredded carrots
3 eggs, separated
3/4 c. shredded cheddar cheese
1/2 tsp. salt
1/8 tsp. pepper
1/8 tsp. cream of tartar
3 Tbsp. flour

Combine rice, carrots, egg yolks, flour, cheese, salt, and pepper in a bowl. In a separate bowl, beat egg whites with cream of tartar until stiff but not dry. Gently fold egg whites into rice mixture to combine. Add a tablespoon of oil to a non-stick skillet or spray with cooking spray. Heat over medium heat. Spoon 2 tablespoons of batter onto skillet for each pattie. Flatten slightly. Cook, turning once, until both sides are brown. Repeat with remaining batter.

BAKED BEAN CASSEROLE

1 can pork and beans
1 can kidney beans
1 can lima beans
1/2 lb. hamburger, browned
1/2 c. brown sugar
3/4 c. catsup
1/4 c. minced onion
2 Tbsp. mustard

Mix together and bake for 1 hour.

Mrs. Mabel Yoder

WESTERN BEANS

4 to 5 bacon strips, diced
1 lg. onion, chopped
1/3 c. dry lentils
1 1/3 c. water
2 Tbsp. ketchup
1 tsp. garlic powder
3/4 tsp. chili powder
1/4 tsp. dried red pepper flakes
1/2 tsp. ground cumin
1 bay leaf
16 oz. whole tomatoes with liquid, chopped
15 oz. pinto beans, drained
16 oz. kidney beans, drained

Lightly fry bacon. Add onion. Cook until transparent. Stir in remaining ingredients. Cook over medium heat for 45 min. or until lentils are tender, stirring once or twice. Remove bay leaf before serving. Yield: 8 to 10 servings.

CALICO BEANS

1 lb. bacon
2 lbs. hamburger
2 cans kidney beans
2 cans pork and beans
1 can lima beans
1 can butter beans
2 c. brown sugar
2 c. catsup
4 tsp. mustard
4 Tbsp. vinegar
1 small onion

Fry bacon and hamburger. Drain fat. Add other ingredients and bake at 350° for 2 hours.

SCALLOPED CORN

1 can creamed corn
1 c. sour cream
1 can whole corn, undrained
1 box jiffy corn muffin mix

Mix altogether and stir. Pour into a greased casserole dish. Lay 1 stick oleo over top. Bake at 350° for 1 hr. or until golden.

BAKED CREAMED CORN

1 lg. can creamed corn
2 eggs, beaten
1 1/2 c. milk
1 c. cracker crumbs
2 Tbsp. butter
3/4 c. shredded cheese
2 Tbsp. grated onion
1 tsp. salt

Mix altogether and bake at 350° for 1 hr.

CABBAGE CASSEROLE

1 head cabbage
1 lb. hamburger
1 onion
1/2 c. uncooked rice
2 cans tomato soup
1 1/2 cans water

Chop cabbage and layer in bottom of a casserole dish. Brown hamburger and onion and put on top of cabbage. Sprinkle uncooked rice over hamburger. Pour tomato soup and water over top of everything. Bake 2 hours at 350°.

Mrs. Ora Lena Miller

CAJUN CABBAGE

1 lb. ground beef
2 small onions, chopped
6 c. cabbage, chopped
1 1/4 c. uncooked long-grain rice
14 1/2 oz. can stewed tomatoes
8 oz. tomato sauce
1 c. water
1 tsp. sugar
1 tsp. cajun seasonings
1 tsp salt
1/2 tsp. pepper

In a large Dutch oven, brown hamburger. Add onions and cook until transparent. Add the cabbage, rice, tomatoes, tomato sauce, water, sugar, and seasonings. Cover and bake at 375° for approximately 1 hr. or until cabbage is tender. Yield: 10 to 12 servings.

SOUR KRAUT (to can)

2 qts. shredded cabbage
1 Tbsp. salt
boiling water

Fill jar with cabbage. Put salt on top and fill jars with boiling water. Close with ZINC lids and rubber ring.

Nora Yoder

~ *The way to gain a good reputation is to try to be, what you desire to be.* ~

DANDELION

1/2 lb. bacon, fried
5 hard boiled eggs, sliced
onions, fried in
bacon grease
SAUCE:

Brown 3 Tbsp. flour in bacon grease. Add milk for right consistency and thickness. Stir in 1 c. brown sugar, 3 Tbsp. vinegar, 1 tsp. mustard and a pinch of salt.

Wash and cut up dandelion to suit your taste and add to sauce with bacon, onions, and eggs. Serve immediately over mashed potatoes. Delicious!

Mrs. Mary Ellen Wengerd

My Favorite Recipes:

My Favorite Recipes:

Soups, Salads, and Dressings

CHICKEN NOODLE SOUP

1 broiler fryer chicken, cut up
2 qts. water
1 onion, chopped
2 chicken bouillon cubes
2 celery sticks, diced
2 carrots, diced
2 med. potatoes, peeled and diced
1 tsp. salt
1/4 tsp. pepper
1 1/2 c. lima beans

NOODLES:
1 c. all-purpose flour
1 egg, beaten
1 tsp. butter, softened
1/4 tsp. baking powder
2 to 3 Tbsp. milk
1/2 tsp. salt

In a large kettle, cook chicken in water. Cool broth and skim off fat. Dice chicken, add to broth with remaining ingredients except noodles. Bring to a boil. Reduce heat and simmer, uncovered, until vegetables are tender. For noodles, place flour on a bread board or a counter top and make a well in the center. In a small bowl, stir together remaining ingredients, pour into well. Work the mixture with your hands. Fold flour into wet ingredients until dough can be rolled into a ball. Knead for 5 to 6 min. Cover and let set for 10 min. On a floured surface, roll dough into a square, 1/16 to 1/8" thick. Cut into 1/4" wide strips. Cook noodles in boiling salt water for 2 to 3 minutes or until done. Drain and add to soup just before serving. Yield: 4 to 6 servings.

EASY POTATO SOUP

8 bacon strips, cut up
1 small onion, chopped
1 1/2 to 2 c. leftover mashed potatoes
10 3/4 oz. can cream of mushroom soup
1 to 2 soup cans of milk
1/2 tsp. salt
dash of pepper
2 Tbsp. chopped parsley

Brown bacon until crisp. Remove and drain on paper towel. Add onion to drippings in pan and saute 2 to 3 min. Drain off fat. Meanwhile, in a 3 qt. saucepan, mix cold mashed potatoes and soup until smooth. Add milk gradually to desired consistency, stirring constantly. Add bacon and onions. Season with salt, pepper, and parsley. Heat through. Yield: 3 to 4 servings.

CHEESY VEGETABLE SOUP

2 1/2 c. cubed potatoes	1 c. chopped celery
10 oz. pkg. mixed vegetables	1 lg. onion
2 - 10 oz. cans chicken soup	2 qts. chicken broth
1 lb. velveeta cheese	

Cook vegetables in chicken broth. Add soup and cheese. Heat.

Mrs. Nettie Miller

QUICK VEGETABLE SOUP

1 1/2 lb. ground beef	20 oz. frozen mixed veg., thawed
1/3 c. instant minced onion	1 tsp. sugar
46 oz. tomato juice	1/4 tsp. pepper
2 beef bouillon cubes	

In dutch oven or soup kettle, brown ground beef with onion. Drain. Add remaining ingredients. Bring to a boil, reduce heat and simmer 20 to 30 minutes, or until vegetables are tender. Yield: 10 to 12 servings. (10 cups)

Mrs. Joan Mast

HEARTY HAMBURGER SOUP

1 lb. ground beef	1 1/2 tsp. salt
2 Tbsp. butter	2 c. tomato juice
1 c. carrots, diced	4 c. milk, heated
1 c. potatoes, diced	1/4 c. flour
1 c. chopped onions	

Brown hamburger. Meanwhile cook all the vegetables. Mix flour with hot milk. Add hamburger. Drain vegetables, and add salt, butter, and tomato juice. Add hamburger mixture to vegetables. Simmer a little longer and serve.

Mrs. Ada Mullet

~ When you can't see the bright side, polish the dull side. ~

HEARTY HAM SOUP

1 c. potatoes, diced	1 qt. milk
1/4 c. onions, chopped	1 1/2 tsp. chicken base
1 c. carrots, sliced	1/4 c. margarine
1/2 c. celery, chopped	American cheese
1 1/2 c. ham, cut up	

In a saucepan cook carrots, celery, onions, potatoes, butter and chicken base in enough water to cover vegetables until tender. Add ham and milk, bring to a boil and thicken with a thickening consisting of cornstarch and water to make a paste. Add cheese.

Clara Miller

EASY BROCCOLI SOUP

1 stick oleo	2 to 3 c. cooked broccoli
1/2 c. flour	1 1/2 qt. milk
2 to 3 c. milk	velveeta cheese
1 Tbsp. chicken base	

Melt oleo and add chicken base, flour and immediately add 2 to 3 c. milk. Cook until it thickens, stirring constantly. Add velveeta cheese to your liking. Stir until melted. Meanwhile heat 1 1/2 qt. milk in larger saucepan. Mix cooked broccoli with hot milk and add everything together. Keep on low heat until ready to serve.

CREAM OF BROCCOLI SOUP

6 Tbsp. butter	1 can cream of chicken soup
5 Tbsp. flour, rounded	salt and pepper
1 Tbsp. onion, minced or chopped	1/2 lb. velveeta cheese
	3/4 lb. broccoli, cooked
13 3/4 oz. (1 can) College Inn Chicken broth	fine cooked noodles
2 c. milk	

Saute onions in butter. Blend in flour. Gradually add soup, milk, and broth. Make good and hot, then add velveeta cheese. Add broccoli. Fine cooked noodles may be added as much as you wish.

Mrs. Joan Mast

~ *Flattery is one thing that even turns a head on a stiff neck.* ~

CHILI SOUP

2 lbs. hamburger
4 Tbsp. brown sugar
4 Tbsp. flour
1 can pork and beans
1 can tomato soup
1 qt. tomato juice
taco seasoning
salt to flavor

Fry together hamburger, sugar, flour, and pork and beans. Add rest of ingredients.

Mrs. Laura Miller

CREAMY TOMATO SOUP

3 Tbsp. butter
2 1/2 Tbsp. flour
3 c. strained tomatoes, or juice
1 Tbsp. minced onion
1/4 tsp. celery salt
1 Tbsp. sugar
2 tsp. salt
1 qt. milk
1/8 tsp. pepper

Melt butter in top of double boiler. Add flour, salt, pepper, and celery salt. Add milk gradually and stir until thickened. In a separate pan heat tomatoes and minced onion. Cook until onion is soft, then strain. Add tomatoes to milk, slowly. Stir well. If milk and tomatoes are both near boiling point and tomatoes are added slowly, this will not curd. Beat briskly with an egg beater if it happens to curd. Yield: 6 servings.

BUTTERY ONION SOUP

2 c. chopped onions
1/2 c. butter or margarine
1/4 c. all-purpose flour
2 c. chicken broth
2 c. shredded cheese
salt and pepper
croutons, optional
2 c. milk

In a large kettle saute onions in butter over low heat until tender and transparent, about 25 min. Cook and stir over medium heat until bubbly. Cook and stir for 1 more minute, reduce heat to low. Add cheese and stir constantly until melted. (Do not boil) Season with salt and pepper. Serve with croutons if you wish. Yield: 6 servings.

~ *No matter how far money goes, it still can't go as far as the next paycheck.* ~

CHEESY CHICKEN CHOWDER

3 to 4 c. chicken,
  cooked & cut up
1 qt. chicken broth
1 qt. milk
4 Tbsp. butter
2 c. velveeta cheese
1 tsp. salt
3/4 c. flour
2 c. peas, carrots, &
  potatoes, cooked
1 Tbsp. chicken base

Cook together broth, milk, butter, flour, salt, and 1/4 tsp. pepper. Add cheese to melt. Last add cut up vegetables and chicken.

Mrs. Martha Schlabach

FISH AND CHEESE CHOWDER

1 lb. fish fillets, fresh or froz.
2 Tbsp. butter
6 Tbsp. chopped onion
1 c. chopped carrots
6 Tbsp. chopped celery
1/4 c. flour
1/2 tsp. salt, optional
dash of paprika
2 (10 oz.) cans chicken
  broth, undiluted
1 c. grated cheese

Cut fish in 1" cubes. Melt butter in a large saucepan. Add onions, carrots, and celery. Cook until onion is transparent. Blend in flour, salt, and paprika. Cook 1 min., stirring constantly. Gradually add chicken broth and milk. Cook until thickened, stirring constantly. Add fish, simmer until fish flakes easily, (5 min. for fresh, 10 for frozen). Add cheese, stir until melted. Yield: 2 1/2 qts.

TORTILLA SOUP

1/2 c. chopped green pepper
1/2 c. chopped onion
1/2 tsp. ground cumin
1 Tbsp. margarine
2 (13 3/4 oz.) chicken broth
  (College Inn)
1 c. frozen or canned corn
2 c. crushed tortilla chips
3/4 c. Monterey Jack cheese
12 oz. jar thick &
  chunky salsa

In medium saucepan, over medium heat, cook pepper, onion, and cumin in margarine until tender. Add broth, salsa and corn. Cover and heat to a boil. Reduce heat and simmer for 5 min. Divide chips and cheese among 6 individual serving bowls. Pour soup over chips and cheese and serve immediately.

LIME SALAD

2 (3 oz.) pkgs. lime jello, dry
20 oz. can crushed, drained pineapple
miniature marshmallows
1 c. cool whip
1 container cottage cheese

Mix all ingredients and refrigerate before serving.

QUICK FRUIT SALAD

2 unpeeled apples, diced
1 c. chopped celery
1 c. seedless raisins
1/2 c. nuts
1/2 c. miracle whip
2 Tbsp. sugar
1 c. miniature marshmallows

Stir together sugar and miracle whip. Pour over rest of ingredients and mix. Chill one hour before serving.

INDIANA SALAD

1st layer:
- 2 pkgs. lime jello, prepared
- 1 can crushed pineapple, drained

2nd layer:
- 4 c. whipped topping
- 8 oz. cream cheese

3rd layer:
- 1 1/2 c. pineapple juice
- 1 c. sugar
- pinch of salt

Bring to a boil and stir in 3 egg yolks mixed with 3 Tbsp. clear jel or cornstarch. When almost cool put on top of second layer.

Mrs. Ada Mullet, Mary Beth Troyer

ORANGE DANISH

4 c. water
1/2 c. clear jel
1 1/4 c. sugar
1 pkg. orange kool-aid

Cool. Add grapes, pineapples chunks, and peach slices. Chill. Add sliced bananas just before serving.

Barbara Troyer

*~ A man of words and not of deeds,
is like a garden full of weeds. ~*

RIBBON SALAD

Bottom layer:
1 pkg. lime jello, prepared
Crushed pineapples as desired
Second layer:
1 pkg. orange jello, prepared
Cool and jell slightly. **Mix together 8 oz. cream cheese and 1 c. Rich's topping, whipped.** Add to jello.
Third layer:
1 pkg. cherry jello, prepared
Let each layer set before adding another.

Mrs. Wilma Hochstetler

CREAM CHEESE SALAD

8 oz. cream cheese	1 pkg. lime jello
16 marshmallows	1 pkg. orange jello
1 c. whipped cream	1 c. chopped nuts
1 c. crushed & drained pineapple	

Mix lime jello as directed on box. Pour 1/2 of lime jello in the bottom of a dish and let set until hard. Mix cream cheese, marshmallows and remaining lime jello. Melt altogether. Let set until stiff. Beat and add whipped cream, nuts and pineapple. Mix and pour on top of set lime jello. Mix orange jello and pour over this. Chill and serve.

TAPIOCA

8 c. boiling water	1 pkg. instant vanilla pudding
1 c. pearl tapioca	
1/2 tsp. salt	6 oz. pkg. strawberry jello
	1 c. sugar

Cook water and tapioca together slowly for 15 to 20 min. Mix together rest of ingredients and then add to tapioca. Cook 1 min. Cool. Blend in cool whip and miniature marshmallows.

Mrs. Sevilla Miller

~ You can win more friends with your ears than with your mouth. ~

TAPIOCA

8 c. boiling water
1 c. pearl tapioca

Cook slowly for 15 to 20 min. or until tapioca is clear. Mix together the following and add to tapioca.

1 sm. pkg. instant vanilla pudding
6 oz. pkg. jello
1 c. sugar

Add to tapioca and cook for 1 min. Cool and add whipped cream.

Mrs. Nettie Miller

7 - UP SALAD

2 pkg. lemon jello
2 c. boiling water
2 large bananas
2 c. 7 - Up
1 c. crushed pineapple
1 c. mini. marshmallows

TOPPING:

1/2 c. sugar
2 Tbsp. flour
1 egg
2 Tbsp. butter
1 c. pinapple juice
1 c. whipped cream

Prepare jello in usual manner. Add other ingredients. Chill until firm. Add topping by blending flour and sugar, and a little bit of juice; blend with eggs. Heat remaining juice to boiling, add to mixture. Return to heat and cook until thick, stirring constantly. Remove from heat, add butter and cool. Fold in whipped cream.

Nora Yoder

KOOL WHIP SALAD

1 can crushed pineapple
1 c. white sugar
6 Tbsp. water

Dissolve water with 2 pkgs. Knox gelatin. Bring to a boil. Cool. After cooled add the following ingredients.

2 lg. carrots, shredded fine
1 c. celery, cut fine
1 c. cottage cheese
1 c. nuts
1 c. margarine
1 carton cool whip

Stir together and let set.

Barb Byler

~Swallow your pride occasionally, it's not fattening. ~

RAINBOW SALAD

1 pt. sour cream
3 oz. cherry jello
3 oz. lemon jello
3 oz. orange jello
3 oz. strawberry jello
6 oz. lime jello
1 1/2 c. cold water
6 c. boiling water

Mix 1 c. boiling water with each package of jello and add 1/3 c. of sour cream. Add 1/4 c. cold water to the remainder 1/2 c. jello. This makes 2 different layers. First layer has sour cream in jello, next layer is plain jello, same flavor. This makes 12 layers. Begin with cherry and strawberry. Put in a clear glass dish. Refrigerate each layer to set before adding next layer.

Mary Anna Troyer

TRIPLE ORANGE SALAD

1 pkg. orange jello
1 pkg. instant pudding
1 box vanilla tapioca pudding
3 c. water

Mix and bring to a boil. Boil a few min. or until tapioca is clear. Cool. Add 2 c. whipped topping and 1 can Mandarin oranges, drained.

Mrs. Ada Mullet

ORANGE SALAD

2 c. flour
1/2 c. brown sugar
1/2 c. nuts
1 c. butter
1 can crushed pineapple
1 c. pineapple juice
1 pkg. orange jello
8 oz. cream cheese
1 c. white sugar

Mix together flour, brown sugar, nuts, and butter. Press in oblong pan and bake for 12 to 15 min. at 350°. Drain pineapple juice into saucepan and bring to a boil. Dissolve orange jello in juice and cool. Cream cream cheese with white sugar. Blend in jello. Stir in crushed pineapple. Chill a can pet milk, whip and mix all together. Put on top of crust and serve.

~ Nothing is all wrong. Even a clock that has stopped running is right twice a day. ~

CRANBERRY SALAD

2 c. sugar
2 c. water
1 bag cranberries
2 c. boiling water
2 (3 oz.) pkgs. gelatin, any flavor
1 c. each nuts & celery, chopped

Combine sugar and 2 c. water and boil for 5 min. Wash cranberries and put in syrup. Boil an additional 5 min. Dissolve gelatin in boiling water. Cool and add to cranberries. Stir in celery and nuts. Chill until set.

Anna Yoder

GREEN SALAD

1 pkg. lime jello
1 c. cottage cheese
1 c. hot water
1 small can crushed pineapple
1 Tbsp. horseradish sauce
1/2 c. chopped nuts

Add hot water to jello. Cool and add rest of ingredients.

Anna Yoder

COTTAGE CHEESE SALAD

1 lb. marshmallows
1/2 c. milk
9 oz. cream cheese
1 pt. cottage cheese
1 c. whipped cream
1 can well drained, crushed, pineapples
chopped nuts

Melt marshmallows and milk in double boiler, add cream cheese and let melt. Blend in cottage cheese, cool and add pineapple and nuts. Fold in whipped cream and pour in mold. Refrigerate.

FROZEN WALDORF SALAD

1 c. sugar
1 c. pineapple juice
1/4 tsp. salt
6 Tbsp. lemon juice
4 eggs, slightly beaten

Cook until thick. Cool and add the following ingredients:

1 c. drained, crushed pineapple
1 c. chopped celery
1 c. chopped nuts
4 apples, diced
2 c. whipping cream

Gently fold into the above mixture. Freeze.

MACARONI SALAD

1 c. miracle whip
1 c. sugar
1/4 c. milk
2 Tbsp. mustard
2 Tbsp. vinegar
1 tsp. salt
dried onion

Mix together and add 1 1/2 to 2 c. cooked macaroni and 6 hard boiled eggs.

Mrs. Nettie Miller

POTATO SALAD

4 c. potatoes, cooked & diced
1/2 c. chopped celery
8 bacon slices, fried and crumbled
1/4 c. Kraft grated parmesan cheese
8 oz. cream cheese
2 Tbsp. chopped onion
1/2 tsp. salt
1/3 c. Kraft Italian dressing

Combine potatoes, celery, bacon, cheese, onion, and salt. Gradually add dressing to softened cream cheese, mixing until well blended. Pour over potato mixture. Mix until well blended.

POTATO SALAD

12 c. potatoes, cooked
12 eggs, cooked
1/2 c. onion
2 c. celery, cut fine
3 c. salad dressing
6 Tbsp. mustard
2 Tbsp. salt
2 1/2 c. sugar
1/4 c. vinegar

Peel cooked potatoes and eggs. Put through salad master. Add rest of ingredients and serve. Note: If vinegar is too strong dilute with water to equal 1/4 c. Can also add just enough mustard to color instead of 6 tablespoons.

Laura Miller, Mrs. Margaret Yoder

~ Ideas are funny little things. They don't work unless you do. ~

POTATO SALAD

12 c. potatoes	1 onion
12 eggs	1 1/2 c. chopped celery
DRESSING:	
3 c. salad dressing	1 1/2 c. white sugar
4 Tbsp. mustard	1/2 c. milk
3 tsp. salt	1/4 c. vinegar

Mrs. Mabel Yoder

WARM TACO SALAD

1 bag flavored tortillas	1 1/2 tsp. pepper
2 lb. hamburger	3 sm. cans tomato sauce
2 small onions	15 oz. can hot chili beans
1 tsp. hot sauce	1/2 tsp. salt
1/2 tsp. minced garlic	

Crumble chips in bottom of a cake pan. Fry hamburger and add the above ingredients. Sprinkle shredded cheese on top of chips, then put hamburger mixture on top of that. Bake at 375° for 30 min. Remove from oven and put 8 oz. sour cream on top. Bake 5 more minutes or until melted. Take out and put shredded lettuce and tomato cubes on top. Serve with taco sauce or 1,000 Island dressing. Yield: 8 to 10 servings.

Note: A good side dish is flavored rice.

Barb Byler

TACO SALAD

1 head lettuce, chopped	1 lg. onion, chopped
1 lb. hamburger	4 med. tomatoes, diced
8 oz. cheddar cheese, grated	1 pkg. Nacho cheese chips
1 small can kidney beans	1 pkg. taco seasoning

Brown hamburger. Add taco seasoning, reserving 1 tablespoon for dressing. Select a large salad bowl allowing enough room to toss salad at serving time. Layer salad ingredients in bowl starting with lettuce and ending with cheese. Cover and refrigerate.

DRESSING:

8 oz. french dressing	1 Tbsp. taco seasoning
1/3 c. sugar	1 Tbsp. taco sauce

Clara Miller, Mrs. Sue Miller

TACO SALAD

1 lb. hamburger
1 pkg. taco seasoning
1 head lettuce, chopped
1 can red beans, drained
8 oz. cheddar cheese
1 pkg. taco chips, crushed
1/3 c. sweet & sour dressing
1 bottle thousand island dressing

Brown hamburger and taco seasoning, reserve 1 Tbsp. for dressing. Mix together lettuce, beans, cheese, and chips. Mix dressings and 1 Tbsp. taco seasoning and pour over salad.

Mrs. Mary Ann Hershberger

BROCCOLI SALAD

1 head broccoli, cut up
1 med. onion, diced
1 head cauliflower, cut up
2 c. cheddar cheese, grated
6 to 12 strips bacon, fried and crumbled
SAUCE:
3/4 c. sour cream
1/2 c. white sugar
3/4 c. mayonnaise
1/4 tsp. salt

Mix sauce ingredients real well. Pour over broccoli mixture. Can be make a day ahead.

Mrs. Naomi Yoder, Mrs. Laura Miller

BROCCOLI SALAD

1 head broccoli
1 head lettuce
2 c. grated cheese
1 lb. bacon, fried & cut up
DRESSING:
1 c. mayonnaise
1 c. sugar
2 Tbsp. vinegar

Add to salad before serving.

Clara Miller

BROCCOLI SALAD

16 strips bacon, crumbled
1 bunch broccoli, cut fine
1 head cauliflower, cut fine
1 c. raisins
1 c. grated cheese
1 c. mayonnaise
4 Tbsp. vinegar
1/2 c. sugar

Put broccoli and cauliflower in cold water for 1/2 hour. Cut fine. Add raisins, cheese and bacon. Mix mayo, sugar, and vinegar together. Pour over salad and mix.

Mrs. Ora Lena Miller

SEVEN LAYER SALAD

Layer in order given:
1 1/2 head lettuce, chopped
1 med. onion, chopped
15 oz. frozen peas, thawed
1 lb. bacon, fried & crumbled
3/4 lb. cheddar cheese, shredded
8 hard boiled eggs, diced

DRESSING:
3 c. miracle whip
1/2 c. white sugar
1/4 c. milk

Nora Yoder

THOUSAND ISLAND DRESSING

1 1/2 qt. salad dressing
3/4 c. pickle relish
3/4 c. catsup
1/2 tsp. salt
1/2 c. sugar

Mix by hand or with mixer. Yield: Approximately 2 qts.
Note: For taco salad add taco seasoning.

Ruby Beachy

SWEET AND SOUR DRESSING

2 c. miracle whip
1 c. white sugar
1/2 c. vegetable oil
1 Tbsp. vinegar
1 Tbsp. mustard
celery seed as desired

Mix miracle whip and sugar. Add remaining ingredients and blend well. A small amount of water may be added if too thick. Good for tossed salads.

Mrs. (Henry) Edna Miller

FRENCH DRESSING

1 c. white sugar
1 c. vegetable oil
3/4 c. ketchup
1/2 c. vinegar
1/4 c. lemon juice
3 Tbsp. grated onion
1 Tbsp. salt
1 tsp. celery seed
1/2 tsp. paprika

Blend together. Cover and refrigerate.

SOUR CREAM DRESSING

2 c. mayonnaise
2 c. buttermilk
1 tsp. parsley flakes
1/2 tsp. celery salt
1/2 tsp. onion salt
1/2 tsp. garlic salt

Shake in a jar. Do not process in blender. Cover and refrigerate.

LAURA'S DRESSING

2 c. white sugar
2/3 c. vinegar
2 tsp. salt
2 tsp. celery seed
1/2 tsp. pepper
1/3 c. salad dressing
1 tsp. mustard
2 c. oil

Add oil last. Beat well.

Anna Yoder

My Favorite Recipes:

My Favorite Recipes:

Desserts

LEMON DELIGHT

First Layer:
1 c. flour, 1 stick oleo, softened and 1/2 c. pecans chopped fine. Mix together and press into an 8" square pan. Bake at 375° for 15 min.

Second Layer:
8 oz. cream cheese, softened, 1 c. powdered sugar, and 1 c. cool whip. Beat together and chill for 15 min. Spread on top of first layer.

Third Layer:
2 pkgs. instant lemon pudding and 3 c. milk. Beat until thick and spread on second layer.

TRY PUDDING DESSERT

Bottom Layer:
1/2 c. flour   2/3 c. chopped nuts
1 1/2 sticks oleo

Mix and press in bottom of a pan. Bake at 350° for 25 min. Cool.

Second Layer:
8 oz. cream cheese   1 c. cool whip
1 c. powdered sugar

Beat together and spread over cooled crust.

Third Layer:
1 pkg. each of chocolate, vanilla and butterscotch instant pudding, prepared.

Spread on cream cheese topping.

~ *The best gifts are tied with heartstrings.* ~

~ *Of all the things you wear your expression is the most important.* ~

FLORIDA PUDDING

1st layer:
1 c. flour   1/2 c. butter
1/2 c. nuts

Mix well. Put in pan and bake until brown. Cool.
2nd layer:
8 oz. cream cheese   1 c. powdered sugar
1 c. cool whip

Mix together and put on first layer.
3rd layer:
2 pkgs. instant pudding, any flavor
3 c. milk

Mix. After pudding is thick spread over second layer. Top with cool whip and nuts.

Mary Anna Troyer

CHOCOLATE PUDDING DESSERT

1 1/4 c. bisquick   1 c. Rich's topping, beaten
1 Tbsp. brown sugar   1 pkg. chocolate pudding
3 Tbsp. oleo, melted   1 1/2 c. milk
1/4 c. chocolate chips   1 pkg. vanilla pudding
1 c. powdered sugar   1 1/2 c. milk
1 pkg. cream cheese, softened nuts

Mix bisquick, brown sugar, oleo and chocolate chips. Bake at 350° for 20 min. Mix powdered sugar and cream cheese together. Add to beaten topping. Spread on cooled crust. Mix chocolate pudding and milk together. Spread on cream cheese mixture. Mix vanilla pudding and milk and spread on chocolate layer. Top with whipped cream and nuts.

CHOCOLATE LOVERS DESSERT

1 chocolate cake mix   fudge topping
1/2 gal. vanilla ice cream   cool whip

Bake cake as directed. Cool. Cut cake in half lengthwise. Put ice cream between layer of cake. Layer with fudge topping and cool whip. Keep frozen till about ready to serve then thaw out.

Mrs. Martha Schlabach

CREAM FILLED CHOCOLATE COOKIE ICE CREAM PIE

16 oz. pkg. oreo cookies, crushed
1/4 c. butter, melted
1/2 gal. vanilla ice cream, softened
10 oz. chocolate fudge topping
12 oz. whipped topping

Mix crushed cookies with melted butter. Press into an oblong pan or 12" pie taker. Spread ice cream over cookies. Pour fudge topping in even layer over ice cream. Spread whipped topping over fudge. Garnish with chocolate curls or small oreo cookies. Put in freezer for 2 hrs.

HOT FUDGE PUDDING

Cream together:
3 Tbsp. oleo
Add:
1 c. flour
1 1/2 tsp. baking powder
1/2 tsp. salt

3/4 c. white sugar

1/2 c. milk
1/2 c. nuts

Put in ungreased pan. Mix 1 c. brown sugar and 1/4 c. cocoa together. Sprinkle over batter. Do not stir. Pour 1 1/4 c. hot water over top of batter and cocoa mixture. Bake at 350°. Serve warm with ice cream or cold with whipped topping.

Susie Yoder and Mrs. Ada Troyer

APPLE GOODIE

1/2 c. sugar
2 Tbsp. flour
1/4 tsp. salt
TOPPING:
1 c. flour
1 c. oatmeal
1 c. brown sugar

1 tsp. cinnamon
1 1/2 qts. sliced apples

1/4 tsp. soda
1/3 tsp. baking powder
2/3 c. butter

Mix sugar, flour, salt and cinnamon, add to apples. Put in a greased pan. Mix topping ingredients until crumbly. Put on apples and pat firmly. Bake at 350° until brown and crust is formed. Serve with milk or ice cream.

Mrs. Esta Miller

APPLE CRISP

1 c. brown sugar
2 tsp. lemon juice
1/4 c. water
1/2 tsp. cinnamon

6 tart apples,
  peeled & sliced
3/4 c. flour
1/4 tsp. salt
6 tsp. butter

Combine 1/2 c. of brown sugar, lemon juice, water and cinnamon in a baking pan. Slice apples into pan and mix. Blend remaining sugar, flour, salt and butter to form crumbs. Spread over apple mixture, pat smooth. Bake at 375° for 40 or 45 min. or until apples are tender and crust nicely brown.

Mrs. Joan Mast

JELLO PUDDING

1 small box jello
1 c. hot water
8 oz. cream cheese
1 c. sugar

1 tsp. vanilla
1 c. whipped cream or
  Rich's topping

Mix jello with 1 c. of hot water. When it starts to set cream together other ingredients and add to jello. Chill until firm. For top layer mix one small box jello as directed on box. Chill and pour over top of first mixture.

Nora Yoder

PUDDING DESSERT

1 box. vanilla pudding mix
8 oz. crushed pineapple
  (with juice)
1 c. miniature marshmallows

1/2 c. chopped nuts
8 oz. cool whip

Mix vanilla pudding mix with pineapple and let stand 5 min. Add marshmallows, nuts and cool whip. Mix well. Pour into a serving dish.

ROAD TO HEAVEN DESSERT

2 sm. pkgs. jello
1 1/2 c. hot water
1 c. whipping cream

1 c. pineapple
1 c. nuts
2 bananas

Mix hot water with jello. Cool until partly set then add whipped cream, pineapple, nuts and sliced bananas.

Anna Yoder

FRUIT PIZZA

CRUST:
1/4 c. butter
1 c. brown sugar
1 egg
1 c. flour
1 tsp. baking powder
1/4 tsp. salt
1 tsp. vanilla

FILLING:
8 oz. cream cheese
1/3 c. sugar
1 tsp. vanilla

TOPPING:
3 c. unsweetened pineapple juice
1/2 c. sugar
2 1/2 Tbsp. clear jell
peaches, oranges, pineapple, strawberries, etc.

Crust: Melt butter, blend with sugar and eggs. Mix flour, baking powder and salt. Mix well and add vanilla. Cover pan with foil. Spread with dough. Bake at 350° for 10 to 12 min. Cool. Remove from foil and return to pan. **Filling:** Combine all ingredients and spread over crust. **Topping:** Cook pineapple juice, sugar, and clear jell until mixture boils. Boil 1 min. Remove from heat and cool. Dip each piece of fruit in mixture before arranging fruit on cream cheese mixture. Note: Double recipe for jelly roll pan.

FRUIT DESSERT

1 c. butter or oleo
1 3/4 c. sugar
4 eggs, beaten
3 c. flour
1 1/2 tsp. baking powder
1 tsp. salt
4 to 6 c. pie filling

Cream oleo, sugar, and eggs. Sift together flour, baking powder, and salt. Add to creamed mixture. Spread half of batter in a cookie sheet (13 x 17). Top with fruit pie filling, any flavor. Spoon the rest of batter on top and spread it over filling. It won't cover completely. Bake at 350° for 35 to 40 min. Drizzle with glaze immediately after removing from oven.

GLAZE:
1 1/2 c. powdered sugar
1 1/2 tsp. butter
2 to 3 Tbsp. milk

Mix powdered sugar, butter and enough milk for a thick glaze.

Mrs. Margaret Yoder

STRAWBERRY SWIRL DESSERT

6 oz. pkg. strawberry gelatin   2 c. boiling water
   Combine and stir until dissolved.
1 med. can crushed pineapple, drained
2 c. sliced strawberries or 16 oz. pkg. frozen strawberries
   Stir in with gelatin mixture. Dot with miniature marshmallows. Let set until firm.
8 oz. pkg. cream cheese   1 c. sweet cream, whipped
   Spread over gelatin and serve.

PRETZEL DESSERT

2 c. crushed pretzels   3 Tbsp. sugar
3/4 c. melted oleo
   Mix together and press into a 9 x 13" pan. Bake at 400° for 8 min. Cool.

FILLING:
8 oz. softened cream cheese   8 oz. cool whip
1 c. sugar
   Cream together cream cheese and sugar. Fold in cool whip. Spread over crust.

TOPPING:
6 oz. strawberry gelatin   2 - 10 oz. pkgs. frozen
2 c. boiling water   strawberries
   Dissolve gelatin in boiling water. Fold in frozen strawberries. Let set about 8 min., allowing strawberries to thaw. Pour over cream cheese mixture. Refrigerate.

RASPBERRY SPECIAL

2 c. pretzel crumbs   9 oz. cool whip
1 c. soft oleo   2 c. pineapple juice
8 oz. cream cheese   2 sm. pkgs. rasp. jello
1 c. sugar   2 pkgs. frozen raspberries
   Mix pretzel crumbs with oleo. Press into a 9 x 13" glass pan and bake at 350° for approximately 10 min. Cool completely. Whip together cream cheese, sugar and cool whip. Spread over cooled crust. Boil together pineapple juice, jello and raspberries. Let mixture gel, then put on top of second layer. Keep refrigerated.

CHERRY DELIGHT
CRUMBS:
1 pkg. crushed graham crackers
4 Tbsp. butter, melted   1 Tbsp. white sugar
CREAM CHEESE MIXTURE:
2 pkg. cream cheese   1 c. powdered sugar
2 eggs, beaten   1 tsp. vanilla

Mix crumbs. Press in pan. Put cream cheese mixture on top. Bake at 350° for 15 min. Cool. Top with 1 can cherry pie filling and cool whip.

Karen Raber

HAWAIIAN PINEAPPLE PUDDING
1 cake mix (yellow or white)   9 oz. cool whip
8 oz. cream cheese   2 c. milk
20 oz. pineapple, drained   3/4 c. coconut
1 box French Vanilla instant pudding

Bake cake in a 9 x 13" pan. Let cool. Soften cream cheese with a little pineapple juice. Blend pudding with milk. Beat cream cheese and pudding together. Spread on cake. Put pineapple over pudding. Top with cool whip and coconut.

Clara Miller

TWINKIE PUDDING
12 twinkies   1 container cool whip
2 lg. pkgs. vanilla   4 c. milk
  instant pudding   nuts
1 lg. can crushed pineapples, drained
2 - 3 sliced bananas, optional

Cut twinkies in half and put in a large pan. Mix milk with pudding and let set awhile. Spread pudding mixture over twinkies, then add pineapples, bananas and cool whip on top. Sprinkle with nuts. Can be made a day ahead.

Mrs. Lizzie Keim

~ *Before you give someone a piece of your mind make sure you can spare it.* ~

FLUFF PUDDING

4 egg yolks, beaten	4 egg whites, beaten
1 c. milk	2 c. Rich's topping, whipped
2 c. white sugar	vanilla
2 pkgs. gelatin	2/3 c. butter
2 pkgs. graham crackers	2/3 c. cold water

Boil first 3 ingredients one minute, stirring constantly. Dissolve gelatin in water. Pour this into hot mixture and set aside until cold. Add beaten egg whites, Rich's topping and vanilla. Let it set, then brown butter and pour over crushed graham crackers. Put in layers.

Elmina Beachy

BAKED CRACKER PUDDING

Desired amount:

vanilla pudding, cooked	melted butter
graham crackers, crushed fine	egg whites

Cover bottom of oblong baking pan with cracker crumbs mixed with butter. Put pudding over that. Top with stiffly beaten egg whites and bake until golden brown.

Nora Yoder

GOODY PUDDING

1/2 stick oleo	1 c. white sugar
8 c. milk, heated	1/2 c. brown sugar
4 Tbsp. cornstarch, level	1/2 tsp. salt
2 Tbsp. flour, level	3 eggs, beaten
2 pkgs. French vanilla pudding (not instant)	1 c. milk

Melt oleo and add 8 c. milk; heat. Stir together rest of ingredients and add to hot milk mixture. Cook until thick. More vanilla pudding may be added. When ready to serve whip 1 c. cream and stir in pudding. Fix in layers with crushed graham crackers. Spread whipped cream on top.

Mrs. Mary Ellen Wengerd

OLD FASHIONED CRACKER PUDDING

3 Tbsp. flour
2 Tbsp. corn starch
1 c. sugar
1 pint milk
2 eggs, separated
1 tsp. vanilla
graham crackers, crushed
bananas, sliced
whipped topping

Cook together first four ingredients. Remove from stove and add 2 egg yolks and vanilla. Beat egg whites and fold in pudding when cold. Layer with graham crackers, bananas and topping.

Anna Yoder

HEATH BAR DESSERT

4 c. graham or Ritz crackers, crushed
1/4 c. butter
2 pkgs. instant vanilla pudding
2 c. milk
1 qt. softened vanilla ice cream
1 container cool whip

Mix cracker crumbs and butter together and press into a dish. Reserve some crumbs for top. Combine pudding, milk and ice cream. Put over crumbs. Top with cool whip, cracker crumbs and crushed candy bars.

Barbara Jean Mullet

ICE CREAM PUDDING

1 pkg. crushed Ritz crackers   1/4 c. oleo

Mix together and press in pan, reserving some for top.

PUDDING:

6 c. vanilla ice cream, softened
2 pkgs. instant vanilla pudding
1 c. milk

Mix milk and pudding. Add ice cream. Spread over crumb mixture, then put reserved crumbs on top.

Karen Raber

~ *Opportunities are seldom labeled.* ~

PISTACHIO PUDDING

1st Part:
1 c. flour   **1/2 c. margarine**
Mix and press in bottom of a pan. Bake at 350° for 15 min. Cool.
2nd Part:
8 oz. cream cheese   **1 c. cool whip**
1 c. powdered sugar
Mix and spread over crust.
3rd Part:
2 pkgs. instant pistachio pudding
3 c. milk
Whip until thickened. Put on second layer and top with cool whip.

Marie Troyer

PISTACHIO PUDDING

1 box pistachio instant pudding mix   **8 oz. cool whip cottage cheese**

Mix pudding mix with cool whip and add cottage cheese as desired. Can also add drained and crushed pineapple.

OREO COOKIE PUDDING

1st layer:
crushed oreo cookies
2nd layer:
8 oz. cream cheese   **1 1/2 c. Rich's topping,**
1 c. powdered sugar   **not whipped**
3rd layer:
1 pkg. chocolate instant pudding, prepared
4th layer:
whipped topping
Sprinkle with crushed oreos.

Mrs. Nettie Miller

*~ Some cause happiness wherever they go;
others whenever they go. ~*

OREO PUDDING

1 pkg. oreos, crushed
2 pkgs. vanilla pudding, prepared
1 1/2 c. whipped topping
8 oz. cream cheese
3/4 c. white sugar

Place crushed cookies in bottom of a pan. Reserve some for top. Mix remaining ingredients and pour on top of cookies. Sprinkle remaining cookies on top.

Mrs. Sue Miller

DIRT PUDDING

CRUST:
Oreo cookies (lg. pkg.)
1/2 c. butter, melted
1/2 c. sugar
PUDDING:
8 oz. cream cheese, softened
1 c. powdered sugar
3 c. milk
1 sm. container cool whip
2 pkgs. instant vanilla pudding

Crust: Crumble cookies and mix with butter and sugar. Put into a 9 x 13" pan. Save 1/2 c. for top. **Pudding:** Whip together cream cheese, powdered sugar, pudding mix, milk, and cool whip. Pour over mixture in pan. Sprinkle remaining cookie crumbs on top. Chill.

Diane Keim

OREO MINT DESSERT

Make 2 days ahead so marshmallows and mints will melt.
CRUST:
20 crushed oreo cookies
FILLING:
16 oz. cool whip
2 c. miniature marshmallows
1 1/4 c. dinner mints, crushed

Put oreo cookies in bottom of a 9 x 12 " cake pan. Mix cool whip, marshmallows and mints together and pour over crust. Sprinkle 8 crushed oreos on top.

Note: I use Ande's chocolate mints.

~ *Trying times are times for trying.* ~

DATE PUDDING

1 c. dates, cut up	1 c. white sugar
1 tsp. soda	1 c. flour
1 tsp. butter	1 egg
1 c. hot water	1/2 c. nuts

Put dates, soda and butter in bowl. Pour hot water over it. Stir and set aside to cool. Add sugar, flour, egg and nuts. Put in a greased pan. Bake at 350° for 40 to 50 min.

SAUCE:

1 stick butter	3 Tbsp. clear jel
1 c. brown sugar	1/2 tsp. maple flavoring
1 pt. water	

Brown butter. Add sugar, water and clear jel. Cook and add maple flavoring. When fixing your date pudding in a dish, layer date pudding, sauce, then whipped cream. Last put whipped cream on top and garnish with sauce.

Ruby Beachy

DATE PUDDING

1 c. chopped dates	1 c. sugar
1 c. boiling water	3/4 c. chopped nuts,
1 tsp. soda	optional
2 eggs	1/4 tsp. salt
1 Tbsp. butter	bananas, sliced
1 c. flour	whipped topping

Pour boiling water over dates and soda. Cool and add all ingredients except for bananas and whipped topping. Bake at 350° for 1/2 hour. Cool and cut in 1" squares. Layer in a serving dish with bananas and whipped topping.

Sarah Yoder

DATE PUDDING

1 c. chopped dates	1 tsp. soda
1 c. boiling water	1/2 c. chopped nuts
1 Tbsp. butter	1 1/2 c. flour
1 c. white sugar	pinch of salt
1 tsp. vanilla	whipped cream

Pour boiling water over dates and soda. Cool. Add other ingredients except for whipped cream. Bake and cut into small pieces. Serve with whipped cream.

Mrs. Wilma Hochstetler

CARAMEL DUMPLINGS

2 Tbsp. butter or oleo
1 1/2 c. brown sugar
1 1/2 c. water
1 1/4 c. all-purpose flour
1/2 c. sugar
2 tsp. baking powder
1/2 tsp. salt
1/2 c. milk
2 Tbsp. butter
2 tsp. vanilla
1/2 c. coarsley chopped, peeled apple

In a skillet heat two tablespoons of butter, brown sugar, and water to boiling. Reduce heat to simmer. Meanwhile mix together all remaining ingredients. Drop by tablespoonful into the simmering sauce. Cover tightly and simmer for 20 min. Do not lift lid. Serve warm with ice cream or cool whip if you wish. Yield: 6 to 8 servings.

LEMON APPLE DUMPLINGS

1 1/2 c. all-purpose flour
1 1/4 tsp. salt, divided
1/3 c. shortening
4 to 5 Tbsp. cold milk
1/2 c. brown sugar
 LEMON SAUCE:
1/2 c. sugar
4 tsp. cornstarch
1 c. water
3 Tbsp. oleo, softened
1/2 tsp. cinnamon
4 med. baking apples peeled and cored
1 egg white, beaten

3 Tbsp. butter or oleo
4 tsp. lemon juice
2 tsp. grated lemon peel

Combine flour and 1 teaspoon salt. Cut in shortening until crumbly. Stir in milk until pastry forms a ball; set aside. Stir brown sugar, butter, cinnamon, and remaining salt to form a paste. Divide and press into center of each apple. Pat any extra filling on outside of apples. Roll pastry into a 14" square. Cut into four 7" squares. Brush edges of pastry with egg white. Fold up corners and pinch to seal. Place in a 9" baking dish. Bake at 375° for 35 to 40 min. Meanwhile, combine sugar and cornstarch in a saucepan. Stir in water. Bring to a boil; boil 2 min. Remove from heat. Stir in remaining ingredients until smooth. Serve warm over dumplings. Yield: 4 servings.

~ Tact is the ability to close your mouth before somebody else wants you to. ~

GOLDEN BROWN APPLE DUMPLINGS

2 c. flour
1 tsp. salt
2 tsp. baking powder
3/4 c. shortening
1/2 c. milk
6 apples

Pare and core apples. Sift flour, salt and baking powder. Cut in shortening. Add milk and stir just until flour is moistened. Roll 1/4" thick. Cut into 5 to 6" squares. Place 1 apple on each square. Sprinkle with sugar and spices. Fold corners and pinch edges. Place 1" apart in a greased pan. Pour the following sauce over dumplings. Bake at 375° for 35 min. Serve hot with ice cream. Serves 6.

SAUCE:

2 c. sugar
2 c. water
1/4 tsp. cinnamon
1/4 tsp. nutmeg
1/4 c. butter

Combine all ingredients except butter. Cook for 5 min. and add butter.

Mrs. Margaret Yoder

ABBY'S RICE PUDDING

2/3 c. uncooked white rice
3 c. boiling water
1/2 tsp. salt
1 Tbsp. vanilla
14 oz. sweet condensed milk
1/4 c. butter or margaine

Cook together for 20 min. Serve. Sinfully delicious!

Anna Yoder

ANGEL FOOD CAKE DESSERT

Bake an **angel food cake** in a regular pan lined with wax paper. Cut cake in 1/2" squares. Mix together **2 c. Rich's topping, 1 c. powdered sugar** and **8 oz. cream cheese.** Put mixture between 2 layers of cake. Cook **a package of danish dessert.** Cool. Add 2 packages frozen or fresh strawberries. Cover cake with strawberry mixture.

Mrs. Laura Miller

~ *One learns manners from those who have none.* ~

ANGEL FOOD CAKE DESSERT

1 sm. angel food cake
1 sm. pkg. instant vanilla pudding
1 pt. vanilla ice cream
1/2 c. milk
1 (6 oz.) pkg. strawberry jello
2 c. boiling water
1 (10 oz.) pkg. frozen strawberries

Tear cake into small pieces and place in a 9 x 13" pan. Combine pudding, ice cream, and milk. Pour over cake. Refrigerate. Combine jello and water, add frozen strawberries. Refrigerate until partially set. Pour on top of pudding layer. Top with cool whip. Refrigerate.

ANGEL FOOD DESSERT

Tear up **1 angel food cake.** Put in bottom of a 9 x 13" pan. Mix **2 packages instant vanilla pudding** and pour over cake. Pour **2 cans pineapple** or **peach pie filling** over pudding. Mix **2 packages dream whip** and **8 oz. package cream cheese** till creamy and pour on top. Sprinkle with **graham cracker** crumbs. Refrigerate several hours.

DELICIOUS CUSTARD

2 Tbsp. oleo or butter
1/4 c. cornstarch
3/4 c. white sugar
1/2 tsp. salt
2 c. milk
2 egg yolks, beaten
1 tsp. vanilla

Melt butter. Add cornstarch, sugar and salt. Gradually add milk and heat to boiling. Stir in egg yolks. Return to heat and cook 2 min., stirring constantly. Add vanilla. Place in serving dish and sprinkle with brown sugar. Serve warm or cold.

Mrs. (Henry) Edna Miller

QUICK BAKED APPLES

4 to 5 apples, peeled & halved
2 Tbsp. butter
2/3 c. brown sugar
whipped cream

Melt butter in skillet. Add brown sugar. Arrange apples face down, enough to fill pan. Cover with tight fitting lid and simmer slowly until apples are tender. Remove apples and place on a platter. Pour juices over top and serve with whipped cream.

PRUNE WHIP

CUSTARD:
- 2 Tbsp. flour
- 1 pt. milk
- 1/2 c. sugar
- 3 egg yolks
- 1 tsp. vanilla

Place this in bottom of a baking dish.
Top with the following:

- 1 c. prunes, finely chopped
- 1/2 c. white sugar
- 3 egg whites, beaten
- 1/2 tsp. soda

Place in oven until brown.

Nora Yoder

CHOCOLATE CHEESECAKE

CRUST:
- 1 1/2 c. graham cracker crumbs
- 6 Tbsp. unsalted butter, melted
- 3 Tbsp. unsweetened cocoa powder
- 3 Tbsp. sugar
- 1/3 c. finely chopped pecans
- 1/4 tsp. ground cinnamon

FILLING:
- 24 oz. cream cheese, softened
- 3/4 c. sugar
- 2 large eggs
- 1 1/2 c. chocolate chips, melted
- 8 oz. sour cream
- 1/3 c. strong brewed coffee
- 2 Tbsp. all-purpose flour
- 1 tsp. vanilla

Preheat oven to 350°. **For crust:** mix ingredients; press into a 9" springform pan to line bottom and 1 1/2" up sides. Bake 8" min. or until lightly browned. Cool on wire rack. **Filling:** cut cream cheese into small pieces. Beat cream cheese, sugar and eggs at high speed until just blended. Beat in remaining ingredients until well blended. Pour into prepared pan. Bake 1 hr. or until filling is set but slightly jiggly. Cool to room temperature on wire rack. In a bowl mix 1/2 c. melted chocolate chips, 2 Tbsp. melted butter and 1 Tbsp. milk. Spread on cake. Cover and chill overnight.

*~ People who do as they please,
seldom please. ~*

LEMON CREAM CHEESE PIE

1 c. sugar
1/2 c. cornstarch
2 1/2 c. cold water
3 eggs yolks, beaten
2/3 c. lemon juice, divided
1/8 tsp. salt
3 Tbsp. butter or margarine
1 can (14 oz.) sweet condensed milk
8 oz. cream cheese, softened
3.4 oz. lemon instant pudding mix
2 pie shells (9") baked
whipped cream
lemon slices

In a saucepan combine sugar and cornstarch. Gradually stir in water, mix until smooth. Cook and stir over medium heat until thickened and clear. Quickly stir in egg yolks. Bring to a boil; boil for 1 min., stirring constantly. Remove from heat and stir in 1/3 c. lemon juice, salt and butter. Cool for several hours. In a mixing bowl blend milk and cream cheese until smooth. Stir in pudding mix and remaining lemon juice. Fold into chilled lemon filling. Spoon into baked pie shells. Refrigerate. Garnish with whipped cream and lemon slices. Yield: 2 pies.

PEACHES AND CREAM CHEESE CAKE

Part 1:
3/4 c. flour
1/2 tsp. salt
1 Tbsp. baking powder
1 egg
3 1/2 oz. pkg. dry vanilla pudding (not instant)
3 Tbsp. butter, softened
1/2 c. milk

Combine in large bowl. Beat for 2 min. Pour in greased 9" pie plate.

Part 2:
Put 1/2 qt. well drained peaches over batter.

Part 3:
8 oz. cream cheese, softened   1/2 c. sugar
3 Tbsp. peach juice

Beat 2 min. Spoon within 1" of edge of batter.

Part 4:
1 Tbsp. sugar   2 tsp. cinnamon

Combine. Sprinkle over part 3 and bake at 350° for 30 to 35 min.

Mrs. Anna Troyer

FROZEN CHEESE CAKE

2 pkg. graham crackers 6 Tbsp. brown sugar
1 c. margarine
Mix together and press into a pan.
8 oz. cream cheese 1 tsp. vanilla
4 eggs, well beaten 1 c. whipped topping
1 c. white sugar

Beat eggs. Add sugar, cream cheese, and vanilla, then add whipped topping. Pour over crust. Freeze. When ready to serve add your favorite fruit topping.

Marie Troyer

CREAM CHEESE PIE

3 oz. lemon jello 8 oz. cool whip
1 c. boiling water 1 c. sugar
8 oz. cream cheese

Mix jello and water together. Cool. Then mix the sugar and cream cheese together. Add cool whip to cream cheese mixture. Combine the cooled jello to the cream cheese mixture. Put in a graham cracker or a baked pie shell and let set. Top with your favorite pie filling.

Ruth Ann Troyer

CREAMY COOL CHEESECAKE

1 c. graham cracker crumbs 3 Tbsp. margarine, melted
1/4 c. sugar

Mix altogether and press into a 9" springform pan.

1 pkg. unflavored gelatin dash of salt
1/4 c. cold water 1/2 c. milk
2 pkg. (8 oz.) cream cheese, 1 c. whipping cream,
  softened whipped
1/2 c. sugar peaches, strawberries,
  blueberries

Soften gelatin in cold water, stir over low heat until dissolved. Combine cream cheese, sugar, salt and milk mixing in electric mixer until well blended. Chill until slightly thickened. Fold in whipped cream. Pour over crust. Chill until firm. Top with fruit.

Mrs. Esta Miller

CHEESE CAKE

2 (8 oz.) cream cheese
1/2 c. sugar
1/2 tsp. vanilla
2 eggs
1 unbaked graham cracker crust

Mix cream cheese, sugar and vanilla until well blended. Add eggs, mix well. Pour into graham cracker crust. Bake at 350° for 40 min. or until center is almost set. Refrigerate 3 hours or overnite.

CRUST:
1 1/4 c. graham cracker crumbs, crushed fine
1/4 c. sugar
6 Tbsp. oleo, melted

Mix altogether and press into a 9" pie plate. Top cooled cheese cake with cherry pie filling or whatever you desire.

Marie Kline

CREAM PUFFS

Put **1 c. water** and **1/2 c. shortening** together in a saucepan; boil up well and add **1 c. sifted flour** immediately, which has been sifted with **1/8 tsp. salt.** Stir vigorously. Remove from heat as soon as mixed, cool. Mix in **3 eggs,** one at a time. Add **2 tsp. baking powder** and beat well. Drop by teaspoonful 1 1/2" apart on a greased baking sheet. Shape round with a wet spoon and bake at 450° for 10 min. Reduce heat to 400° and bake 25 min. or until puffed up, light brown, and thoroughly cooked. Cool. Cut near base of each puff and fill with **ice cream, instant pudding, or cooked vanilla cream pudding.** Sprinkle with **powdered sugar.**

VANILLA CREAM PUDDING:
1/2 c. sugar
2 Tbsp. cornstarch
1/8 tsp. salt
2 eggs, beaten
1 c. scalded milk
1 tsp. butter
1/2 tsp. vanilla

Mix together first 4 ingredients. Pour scalded milk on gradually. Add butter and cook in double boiler until thick, stirring constantly. Add vanilla.

~ *No wise man ever wished to be younger.* ~

PUMPKIN ROLL

1 c. white sugar
2/3 c. pumpkin
3/4 c. flour
3 eggs
1 tsp. salt
1 tsp. soda
1 tsp. cinnamon
3/4 c. chopped walnuts, optional

Mix dry ingredients. Add eggs and pumpkin. Grease a cookie sheet and line with wax paper. Sprinkle with nuts if desired. Bake at 350° for 15 min. Flip baked mixture onto tea towel that is sprinkled with powdered sugar. Remove wax paper immediately and roll in tea towel. Cool.

FILLING:
2 tsp. oleo
8 oz. cream cheese
1 tsp. vanilla
1 c. powdered sugar

Mix all ingredients until creamy. Spread on cooled, unrolled pumpkin cake. Reroll and refrigerate.

Mrs. Esta Miller, Anna Yoder

PUMPKIN LOG

3 eggs
2/3 c. pumpkin
1 c. sugar
1 tsp. baking soda
1/2 tsp. cinnamon
3/4 c. flour

Mix above ingredients together and pour in a greased cookie sheet lined with wax paper. Bake at 375° for 15 min. Turn out onto a towel covered with powered sugar. Pull wax paper off as soon as it is cool enough to touch.

FILLING:
6 Tbsp. flour
3/4 c. brown sugar
vanilla
1 c. hot water
6 Tbsp. butter

Heat flour, sugar and water until thick, stirring constantly. Remove from heat and add butter and vanilla. When cool spread onto cooled cake and roll into a log. Cover with foil and refrigerate.

Mrs. Miriam Miller

~ The tongue can be like a reckless driver - always running people down. ~

JELLY ROLL

1 c. flour	1/4 tsp. salt
1 c. sugar	6 eggs, separated
1 tsp. baking powder	vanilla

Beat egg yolks well, add sugar, beat again, then add flour, baking powder, salt and vanilla. Last add egg whites, well beaten. Bake at 375° for 13 min., in a 12 x 18" sheet pan.

FILLING:

6 Tbsp. flour, level	1 c. hot water
3/4 c. brown sugar	salt

Heat until thick, stirring constantly. Remove from heat. Add 2 Tbsp. butter, vanilla and maple flavoring. Ice cream can also be used to fill the jelly roll.

Mary Beth Troyer

FRIED ICE CREAM

2 Tbsp. butter	1/4 c. brown sugar
1 c. grapenut flakes, crushed	1/2 tsp. cinnamon
1/4 c. chopped nuts	

Melt butter in skillet. Add remaining ingredients. Cook and stir over medium heat until mixture is mixed well. Do not over heat. Cool. Ice cream can be formed in balls with large dipper, then rolled in topping. Can also be put in a dish with ice cream layered between crumbs. 2 batches of topping and 1/2 gallon ice cream fills a square dish. Can be served with honey and whipped cream. Note: A delicious way to top off any Mexican meal.

OUR FAVORITE ICE CREAM

4 eggs, well beaten
Beat in the following:

1 c. powdered sugar	2 sm. pkgs. butter pecan instant pudding
1 c. brown sugar	
1 c. white sugar	6 tsp. vanilla
	2 cans carnation milk

Milk to fill 1 gallon freezer.

Mrs. Laura Miller

HOMEMADE ICE CREAM

Soak **2 pkgs. gelatin** in **1 c. milk**. Scald **7 1/2 c. milk**, then stir in dissolved gelatin mixture. Blend in **2 1/4 or 2 1/2 c. brown sugar, pinch of salt** and **about 3 tsp. vanilla flavoring**. Set aside to cool, put in refrigerator at least half a day. When set or thick take **1 1/2 c. cream,** (canned milk can also be used) and whip it. Whip in **3 egg yolks** and **3/4 c. white sugar**. Mix in with first part.
Makes 1 1/2 gallons.

Mrs. Joan Mast

ICE CREAM

8 c. milk
3 pkgs. vanilla instant pudding
1 pkg. butterscotch instant pudding
8 eggs, separated
1 c. white sugar
1/2 c. brown sugar

5 oz. white Karo
1 tsp. salt
1 tsp. vanilla
1 tsp. maple flavoring
1 can evaporated milk
1 can eagle brand milk

Add enough milk for a 2 gallon freezer.

Mrs. Sevilla Miller

VELVETY ORANGE ICE CREAM

1 c. hot water
1 c. white corn syrup
1/2 c. sugar
2 (3 oz.) pkgs. orange jello
dash of salt

3 Tbsp. lemon juice
1 c. orange juice
2 c. milk
2 c. cream
1 can pineapple, optional

Bring hot water, sugar, and syrup to a boil. Remove from heat and add jello. Stir in fruit juices and let cool. Add milk, cream, and salt. Freeze. Is somewhat like sherbet.

~ The wife who drives from the back seat is no worse than the husband who cooks from the dining room table. ~

My Favorite Recipes:

My Favorite Recipes:

Cakes & Frostings

JOHNNY CAKE

3/4 c. sour milk or buttermilk
1/3 c. maple syrup
3/4 c. cornmeal
1/2 c. flour
1/4 tsp. salt
1/2 tsp. soda

Mix all ingredients. Place in a greased pie pan. Bake at 350° for 25 to 30 min. Serve immediately.

BLACKBERRY CAKE

1 c. jam
3 eggs
1 c. shortening
1 1/2 c. brown sugar
1 tsp. cinnamon
1 tsp. cloves
1 tsp. nutmeg
1 1/2 tsp. soda
1/2 tsp. salt
3 1/2 c. flour
1 1/2 c. sour milk

Cream the shortening and sugar. Add the eggs and beat well. Sift the dry ingredients together. Add alternately with milk. Add blackberry jam last. This makes three 9" layers. Also good for cupcakes.

PEACH CAKE

1/4 c. butter or oleo
1 1/2 c. flour
1 egg
1/2 c. sugar
1/2 c. milk
1 1/2 tsp. baking powder

Mix above as for cake and pour into 2 square cake pans. Pare and slice 6 fresh peaches (or canned) and place the slices close together in rows, pressing gently into cake dough. Sprinkle with sugar and cinnamon and bake in a moderate oven. (350°) Good with sugar and cream.

SOLOMON CAKE

2 eggs
1 c. white sugar
1 c. sour cream
1 tsp. soda
1 tsp. cream of tartar
2 c. flour

Bake in an oblong pan until done.

Anna Yoder

~ Live to learn and you will learn to live. ~

TURTLE CAKE

1 box german choc. cake mix 7 oz. eagle brand milk
14 oz. caramels 6 oz. chocolate chips
1/4 lb. oleo

Mix cake mix as directed on package. Bake half of mixture at 350° for 15 min. Melt together butter, caramels and milk. Cool mixture slightly and pour over baked half of cake. Pour remaining cake batter on top. Sprinkle with chocolate chips. Bake for 25 min. longer.

Karen Raber

HO HO CAKE

Bake **one chocolate cake mix** in a 9 x 13" pan. Cool.

TOPPING NO. 1:
5 Tbsp. flour 1 1/4 c. milk
1/2 c. oleo 1 c. sugar
1 c. crisco

Mix flour and milk in saucepan. Cook until thick, stirring constantly. Cool. Cream together sugar, oleo and crisco. Add flour mixture and beat well. Spread over cooled cake.

TOPPING NO. 2:
1/2 c. oleo 1 egg
3 Tbsp. chocolate 1 tsp. vanilla
2 1/2 Tbsp. hot water 1 1/4 - 1 1/2 c. confectioner's sugar

Melt oleo and cool. Beat egg, vanilla, and hot water. Add sugar and blend well. Pour over first topping and refrigerate.

MIRACLE WHIP CAKE

2 c. flour 1 c. miracle whip
2 tsp. soda 1 tsp. vanilla
1 c. sugar 1 c. cold water
6 Tbps. cocoa

Sift together the first 4 ingredients, then add rest of ingredients. Bake in loaf pan at 375° for about 30 min.

Note: Has to be miracle whip.

BETTER CAKE MIX

3/4 c. flour　　　　　　　　1 tsp. baking powder
1/2 c sugar

Stir ingredients into dry cake mix. Prepare as directed then add the following ingredients:

1/3 c. water　　　　　　　　1 Tbsp. vegetable oil
1 egg

Bake as directions on cake mix.

Ruth Ann Troyer

CHOCOLATE CHIP CAKE

1 1/2 c. shortening　　　　1/2 tsp. soda
1 1/2 c. sugar　　　　　　　1 1/2 c. boiling water
3 eggs　　　　　　　　　　　vanilla
2 1/2 c. flour　　　　　　　　9 oz. chocolate chips
3 Tbsp. cocoa　　　　　　　1/2 c. nuts
1 tsp. salt

Sprinkle chips and nuts on top of batter before baking. No need to ice. Bake at 350° approximately 45 min.

Mrs. Sevilla Miller

SPRINGTIME CHOCOLATE CAKE

1 c. sugar　　　　　　　　　1/4 c. corn oil spread,
1 c. Gold Medal flour　　　　　melted
1/2 c. Hershey's cocoa　　　1/4 c. sour cream
1/2 tsp. soda　　　　　　　　1 egg
1/4 tsp. salt　　　　　　　　　1 tsp. vanilla
1/2 c. water　　　　　　　　　3 c. strawberries
　　　　　　　　　　　　　　　1 1/2 c. powdered sugar

Heat oven to 350°. Lightly spray a 9 x 13 x 2" pan. Sift together sugar, flour, cocoa, soda, and salt. Add water, egg, sour cream, corn oil spread, and vanilla. Beat until smooth. Pour into pan. Bake 18 to 20 min. Just before serving sift powdered sugar over cake. Cut into pieces and spoon 2 Tbsp. strawberries on each piece. Garnish with whipped topping. Low in calories.

Mrs. Anna Troyer

SALAD DRESSING CAKE

2 c. flour
1 c. white sugar
4 tsp. cocoa
2 tsp. soda
1/2 tsp. salt
1 c. water
1 c. salad dressing

Mix everything together and add salad dressing last. Bake at 350° for 30 min.

Mrs. Mabel Yoder

YUMMY CAKE

1 pkg. butter flavored cake mix
11 oz. can mandarin oranges, undrained
1/2 c. salad oil
4 eggs
20 oz. can crushed pineapple, undrained
1 sm. pkg. instant vanilla pudding mix
12 oz. container non-dairy whipped topping
1/2 small pkg. instant vanilla pudding
9 oz. container non-dairy whipped topping

Beat cake mix, oranges, salad oil, and eggs for 3 to 4 min. Bake in three ungreased 8" cake pans. Mix pineapple, small package pudding mix and 12 oz. whipped topping and spread between layers and on top of cake. Refrigerate in a tightly covered container. When ready to serve, mix remaining pudding mix and whipped topping together. Spread on sides of cake. Serve cold.

HOT MILK CAKE

4 eggs
2 c. sugar
2 1/4 c. all-purpose flour
2 1/4 tsp. baking powder
1 tsp. vanilla
1 1/4 c. milk
10 Tbsp. butter or margarine

In a mixing bowl, beat eggs at high speed until thick, about 5 min. Gradually add sugar, beating until mixture is light and fluffy. Combine flour and baking powder. Add to batter with vanilla and beat until smooth. In a saucepan, heat milk and butter just so the butter melts, stirring occasionally. Add to batter, beating until combined. Pour into a greased 9 x 13" baking pan. Bake at 350° for 30 to 35 min. or until cake is done. Yield: 12 to 16 servings.

ROYAL SUNSHINE CAKE

9 eggs, separated
4 1/2 Tbsp. water
1 1/2 c. sugar
1/4 tsp. lemon flavoring
1 1/2 c. flour
1/2 tsp. cream of tartar
1/2 tsp. vanilla flavoring
1/2 c. nuts

Beat egg yolks until light yellow. Add water, sugar and flavorings slowly, continuing to beat until very light and creamy. Fold in flour and nuts. Add a pinch of salt to egg whites and beat until foamy, then add cream of tartar and beat until stiff. Fold into batter. Bake 1 hr. in a tube pan at 325°.

Nora Yoder

CRAZY CAKE

1 1/2 c. flour
1 c. sugar
3 Tbsp. cocoa
1 tsp. soda
1 1/2 tsp. salt
6 Tbsp. vegetable oil
1 Tbsp. vinegar
1 tsp. vanilla

Sift dry ingredients and put in a 10" baking pan. Make three wells in the dry mixture; place oil in one well, vinegar in another well and vanilla in the last well. Pour 1 c. of cold water over all and mix with fork. Bake at 350° for 30 min. Cool and frost.

Mrs. Miriam Miller

CHIFFON CAKE

1 3/4 c. + 2 Tbsp. Robin Hood flour
1 1/2 c. white sugar
3 tsp. baking powder
2 tsp. salt
1/2 c. salad oil
3/4 c. cold water
2 tsp. vanilla
5 egg yolks
1 c. egg whites
1/2 tsp. cream of tartar

Sift together flour, sugar, baking powder, and salt. Make a well and add oil, egg yolks, water, and vanilla. Beat until smooth. Beat egg whites with cream of tartar until it forms very stiff peaks. (Stiffer than meringue). Pour egg yolk mixture gradually over beaten egg whites gently folding in. Do not stir. Pour into ungreased 9" tube pan. Bake 45 min. at 325° then increase heat to 350° for 10 to 15 min. Invert pan to cool cake. Remove from pan. Yield: serves 12.

ICING:
1/4 c. cocoa, 1/4 c. hot water, 1/4 c. white sugar.

Mrs. Wilma Hochstetler

PUMPKIN UPSIDE-DOWN CAKE

3 eggs
1 lg. can pumpkin
1 can evaporated milk
1 3/4 c. sugar
TOPPING:
1 pkg. yellow cake mix
1 1/2 sticks melted oleo

2 tsp. cinnamon
1 tsp. nutmeg
1/2 tsp. ginger

1 c. chopped walnuts

Mix filling ingredients thoroughly and pour into a 9 x 13 x 2" or 3 quart shallow oval casserole dish. Sprinkle dry cake mix evenly over batter and drizzle melted oleo on top. Bake 30 min. at 350°. Sprinkle nuts on top and bake approximately 30 min. longer. Cool thoroughly. Serve with cool whip. Makes 16 servings. 392 calories each.

OLD FASHIONED CHOCOLATE CAKE

3 c. flour
1 1/2 tsp. soda
1 1/2 tsp. baking powder
1/2 tsp. salt
1/2 c. cocoa

3/4 c. shortening
2 c. white sugar
1 tsp. vanilla
1 1/2 c. water
3 eggs, separated

Cream shortening and sugar, blend in egg yolks. Add cocoa and blend in. Add flour, soda, baking powder, and salt alternately with water. Blend until smooth. Add vanilla, then beat egg whites until stiff and fold into batter by hand. Put into 2 - 9" cake pans and bake at 350°.

Elmina Beachy

CAKE DESSERT

1 box lemon or white cake mix
1 pkg. vanilla instant pudding

1 can crushed pineapple
with juice

Bake cake according to package directions. Mix together instant pudding and pineapple. Spread over cake and refrigerate.

~ If you are going to be able to look back and laugh about something, you might as well laugh about it now. ~

OLD FASHIONED HICKORY NUT CAKE

Beat **3 egg whites** until frothy. Gradually add **1/2 c. sugar**. Beat well. Set aside.

1 c. sugar	1/3 c. vegetable oil
2 1/4 c. flour	1 c. water
3 tsp. baking powder	3 egg yolks
1 tsp. salt	1 tsp. vanilla

Sift together sugar, flour, baking powder, and salt. Add other ingredients and beat until smooth. Mix in 3/4 c. hickory nuts and beat in beaten egg whites and sugar. Bake at 350°.

Mrs. Sevilla Miller

STRAWBERRY SHORTCAKE

1 1/2 c. cake flour	6 eggs
1 1/2 tsp. baking powder	1 c. plus 2 Tbsp. sugar
1/2 tsp. salt	1 tsp. lemon extract

Beat eggs until foamy. Gradually add sugar, beating until mixture is thick and stands in soft peaks. (This is important.) Fold in extract and sift dry ingredients together, adding small amounts at a time and folding in carefully each time. Pour into 3 greased pans lined with wax paper. Bake at 350° for 12 to 15 min. Remove from pans immediately and remove wax paper. Serve with fruit or whipped cream.

Mrs. Margaret Yoder

STRAWBERRY SHORTCAKE

2 pt. strawberries, sliced	3 Tbsp. margarine or butter, melted
2/3 c. sugar	1/2 c. milk
2 1/3 c. Bisquick original baking mix	3/4 c. (heavy) whipping cream
3 Tbsp. sugar	

Sprinkle strawberries with 2/3 c. sugar; let stand 1 hour. Heat oven to 425°. Mix baking mix, 3 Tbsp. sugar, margarine, and milk till a soft dough forms. Drop dough into 6 mounds onto an ungreased cookie sheet. Bake 11 to 12 min. or until golden brown. Beat whipping cream in a chilled bowl until stiff. Split shortcakes. Fill and top with strawberries. Top with whipped cream. Yield: 6 servings.

ANGEL FOOD CAKE

Preheat oven to 375°. Have egg whites at room temperature.
1 1/4 c. sifted Swansdown cake flour
1/2 c. sifted sugar   1 1/4 tsp. cream of tartar
1 1/2 c. egg whites   1 tsp. vanilla
1/4 tsp. salt   1 1/3 c. sifted sugar

Measure sifted flour. Add 1/2 c. sugar and sift together 4 times. Combine egg whites, salt, cream of tartar, and vanilla in large bowl. Beat with sturdy beater until moist peaks form. Add rest of sugar in 4 additions, folding with large spoon each time, turning bowl often. Pour into an ungreased tube pan. (Have pan warm.) Bake for 35 to 40 min. For chocolate cake add 2 tsp. cocoa. For a colored cake add a few teaspoons any flavor jello, taking out as much sugar as jello you put in.

Alma Hershberger

PUMPKIN CAKE BARS

4 eggs, well beaten   1 tsp. cinnamon
2 c. cooked pumpkin   1/2 tsp. cloves
1 1/2 c. sugar   1 yellow cake mix
1/4 tsp. salt   1/2 c. melted butter
1 tsp. ginger   1 c. chopped pecans

Mix eggs, pumpkin, sugar, salt, ginger, cinnamon and cloves together. Pour into a 9 x 13" pan. Sprinkle dry cake mix on top. Drizzle melted butter over mix. Spread nuts over all. Bake at 325° for 1 hr. and 20 min. Cover loosely with foil the first half of cooking time to keep from browning too soon. Cut into squares and serve with whipped cream. Yield: 24 bars.

Mrs. Joan Mast

~ Some things are hard to remember, somethings are hard to forget, but don't forget to remember, and remember not to forget. ~

QUICK GINGERBREAD

1 c. sifted flour	1/2 c. sugar
1/2 tsp. salt	1/3 c. soft shortening
1/2 tsp. nutmeg	1/2 c. molasses
1/2 tsp. cloves	1/2 c. warm water
1/2 tsp. allspice	1 tsp. soda
1/2 tsp. baking powder	1/4 c. boiling water
2 1/2 tsp. ginger	1 egg
1 tsp. cinnamon	

Sift flour, spices, baking powder and sugar together into mixing bowl. Add shortening, molasses and warm water. Beat 2 min. with electric beater. Dissolve soda in 1/4 c. boiling water then add to mixture. Add egg and beat 1 min. Pour into greased and floured pan. Bake at 350° for 35 to 40 min.

Mrs. Margaret Yoder

ZUCCHINI CUPCAKES

3 eggs, beaten	2 c. white sugar
2 c. grated zucchini	2 tsp. vanilla
1 c. vegetable oil	1 3/4 c. flour
1 c. coconut	1/4 c. whole wheat flour
1 c. quick oats	1/2 tsp. baking powder
2 tsp. baking soda	1/2 tsp. salt
1 c. chopped nuts	

Blend eggs, sugar, vanilla, zucchini, and vegetable oil. Add flour, oats, soda, salt, and baking powder. Mix well and stir in coconut and nuts. Fill baking cups and bake at 350° for 25 min. Yield: 28 cupcakes.

Sarah Yoder

~Friends are made by many acts - and can be lost by just one. ~

POUND CAKE

6 eggs
2 3/4 c. sugar
1 tsp. vanilla
3 c. all-purpose flour
1 Tbsp. baking powder
1/4 tsp. salt
1 pt. heavy cream

In a mixing bowl, beat eggs until a pale yellow. Gradually beat in sugar and vanilla, mixing until sugar is dissolved. Combine flour, baking powder and salt. Add to batter alternately with cream. Pour into a greased 10" tube pan. Bake at 350° for 60 to 70 min. or until cake tests done. Cool in pan 15 min. before removing to a wire rack. Yield: 12 to 16 servings.

OATMEAL CAKE

1 1/2 c. boiling water
1 c. quick oats
1 c. white sugar
1 c. brown sugar
1/2 c. shortening
1 tsp. vanilla
2 eggs
1 1/2 c. flour
1 tsp. soda
1/2 tsp. salt
1/2 tsp. cinnamon

Pour boiling water over oats. Let cool. Mix sugars, shortening and eggs together. Add rest of ingredients and mix with oats.

FROSTING:
1/2 c. oleo
1 c. brown sugar
1/4 c. evaporated milk
1 tsp. vanilla
1 c. nuts
1 c. coconut

Cook first 3 ingredients together, stirring constantly, about 8 min. Add rest of ingredients. Pour over hot cake and toast quickly.

Mrs. Ida Miller, Linda Miller

~Some people expect it to rain when they thunder. ~

*~ What sunshine is to flowers,
smiles to humanity. ~*

LAZY DAISY CAKE

2 c. all-purpose flour	2 c. sugar
2 tsp. baking powder	2 tsp. vanilla
1/2 tsp. salt	1 c. milk
4 eggs	2 Tbsp. butter

  Mix baking powder and salt to flour and blend. Beat eggs until thick and light colored. Add sugar gradually. Continue to beat until blended. Stir in vanilla. Heat milk and butter until scalding. Beat into egg mixture quickly. Add blended dry ingredients to egg mixture a little at a time, mixing well. Pour into a well greased 9 x 13" oblong pan. Bake at 350° for 35 to 40 min. Spread hot cake with broiled coconut topping.

BROILED COCONUT TOPPING:

1/3 c. butter, softened	3 Tbsp. light cream or milk
3/4 c. brown sugar	1 c. coconut or 1 c. nuts

  Spread over warm cake. Put in broiler for 2 - 4 min.

Clara Miller

WALNUT WONDER COFFEE CAKE

1 c. soft oleo	3 c. flour
1 1/2 c. white sugar	1 1/2 tsp. soda
3 eggs	1/2 tsp. salt
1 1/2 c. sour milk	1 1/2 tsp. baking powder
2 Tbsp. salad dressing	1 1/2 tsp. vanilla

  Add salad dressing to sour milk. Cream sugar, oleo, flour, soda, baking powder, and salt. Add eggs and milk alternately with flour mixture, and vanilla. Bake in 2 small cookie sheets. Mix topping and sprinkle over dough. Put filling between layers.

TOPPING:

1/3 c. brown sugar	1/4 c. white sugar
1 tsp. cinnamon	1 c. chopped nuts

FILLING:

4 3/4 c. powdered sugar	1/2 c. white sugar
1/2 tsp. salt	4 Tbsp. water
2 egg whites, beaten	

  Boil white sugar and water 1 min. Add to above ingredients. Mix and add 3/4 c. crisco.

Mrs. Mary Ellen Wengerd

CHERRY COFFEE CAKE

1 c. oleo	3 c. flour
1 1/2 c. white sugar	1 1/2 tsp. baking powder
4 eggs	1/2 tsp. salt
1 tsp. vanilla	1 can cherry pie filling

Cream oleo and sugar. Add eggs one at a time. Beat well after each. Add vanilla, sifted flour, baking powder, and salt. Spread 2/3 of dough in a large greased jelly roll pan. (10 1/2 x 12) Cover with pie filling and spoon the rest of dough on top. Dribble with glaze.

GLAZE:
1 1/2 c. powdered sugar, 2 Tbsp. oleo.
Add warm milk till right consistency.

Iva Yoder

WONDER WONDER COFFEE CAKE

2 c. flour	Crumbs:
1 tsp. baking powder	1/2 c. brown sugar
1 tsp. soda	1/4 c. white sugar
1/2 tsp. salt	1 tsp. cinnamon
1 c. oleo, softened	1 c. chopped nuts, optional
1 c. sugar	
1. sour milk	
2 eggs	
FILLING:	
2 c. powdered sugar	1 1/2 c. crisco
2 egg whites, beaten	1 Tbsp. vanilla

BLUEBERRY BRUCKLE COFFEE CAKE

4 c. flour	1/2 c. shortening
1 1/2 c. sugar	1 1/2 c. milk
5 tsp. baking powder	2 eggs
1 1/2 tsp. salt	4 c. blueberries

Mix together all ingredients except blueberries. Beat vigorously for 1/2 min. Carefully stir in blueberries. Spread half of batter in a greased pan. Sprinkle half of the following topping over batter. Add remaining batter and sprinkle rest of topping over top. Bake at 350° for 45 to 50 min.

TOPPING:

2 c. sugar	1 tsp. cinnamon
2/3 c. flour	1/2 c. oleo

Mrs. Margaret Yoder

CINNAMON PECAN COFFEE CAKE

1 stick margarine
1 c. sugar
2 eggs
1 tsp. vanilla
1 c. sour cream
1 1/2 c. flour
1 tsp. soda

CRUMBS:
1/2 c. brown sugar
1/2 c. chopped pecans
2 tsp. cinnamon

Cream together margarine and sugar. Beat in eggs and mix well. Add vanilla, sour cream, flour, and soda. Pour 1/2 of batter in a 9" pan and top with half of crumbs. Spoon on remaining batter and sprinkle with rest of crumbs. Bake at 350° for 20 min.

Laura Miller

CREAM FILLED COFFEE CAKE

1 c. milk
1 tsp. salt
2 eggs
1/4 c. warm water
1/2 c. white sugar
1/2 c. oleo
1 Tbsp. dry yeast
3 1/2 c. flour

Scald milk then add salt, sugar, and oleo. Beat eggs in large bowl. Add milk mixture. Dissolve yeast in warm water and add to the above mixture. Mix in flour and let rise overnight. Next morning put dough in 3 pie pans. Spread crumbs on top and let rise. Bake at 325° for 15 min. Cool and split each cake. Fill with filling.

CRUMBS:
1/2 c. brown sugar
1/4 c. butter
1/2 c. flour

FILLING:
2 c. powdered sugar
1 c. crisco
2 tsp. vanilla
4 Tbsp. flour
2 egg whites

Mrs. Naomi Yoder

~ *Futility is two bald headed men fighting over a comb.* ~

~ *Stretching the truth won't make
it last any longer.* ~

SOUR CREAM COFFEE CAKE

TOPPING:
1/3 c. brown sugar
1/4 c. white sugar
2 tsp. cinnamon
1/2 c. chopped pecans

CAKE:
1/2 c. butter
3 eggs
1 tsp. vanilla
1 tsp. soda
1/4 tsp. salt
1 c. sugar
8 oz. sour cream
2 c. flour
1 tsp. baking powder

Cream butter and sugar in bowl, add eggs, sour cream and vanilla. Combine flour, baking powder, soda, and salt. Add to batter and egg mixture. Beat until combined. Pour half of the batter into a 9 x 13" cake pan. Sprinkle with half the topping mixture. Repeat. Bake at 325° for 40 min.

Barb Byler

TEXAS SHEET CAKE

2 sticks oleo
1 c. water
4 Tbsp. cocoa
2 c. sugar
2 c. flour
1 tsp. vanilla
1/2 tsp. salt
1 tsp. soda
2 eggs
1/2 c. sour cream or buttermilk

Melt oleo in saucepan. Add water and cocoa. Bring to a boil. Cool and add the rest of ingredients. Pour into a greased cookie sheet. Bake at 350° for 15 to 20 min.

ICING:
1/2 c. oleo
4 Tbsp. cocoa
6 Tbsp. milk
1 lb. powdered sugar
1/2 c. nuts
1 tsp. vanilla

In a saucepan melt oleo, cocoa, and milk. Bring to a boil. Add remaining ingredients. Spread on cake as soon as it is removed from oven.

Anita Troyer

~ *As long as there are math tests, there will be prayer in schools.* ~

TEXAS SHEET CAKE

1 c. water	1/2 tsp. salt
1/2 c. oleo	2 eggs
4 tsp. cocoa	1 tsp. soda
2 c. flour	1/2 c. buttermilk
2 c. brown sugar	

Boil water, oleo and cocoa in a saucepan. Remove from heat and add flour, sugar, and salt. Beat eggs and blend in soda and buttermilk. Add to other mixture. Bake on a large cookie sheet at 350° for around 18 min.

Mrs. Wilma Hochstetler

WHITE TEXAS SHEET CAKE

2 1/4 c. flour	2 sticks margarine
2 c. white sugar	3 eggs
2 tsp. baking soda	1/2 c. buttermilk or
1 tsp. salt	sour milk

Combine flour, sugar, soda, and salt. Place margarine in a saucepan with 1 c. water and bring to a boil. Combine eggs and buttermilk, add to margarine then pour into flour mixture. Mix until blended. Pour into large cookie sheet with rim. (Batter will be thin.) Bake at 375° for 20 min.

FROSTING:

Bring **1 stick margarine** and **3 Tbsp. milk** to a boil. Gradually add **1 pound powdered sugar** with **one teaspoon vanilla** and mix well. Spread on cake while warm. Sprinkle with **chopped nuts.**

~ It's called "cold cash" because it's never in your pocket long enough to get warm. ~

~ Who gossips to you will gossip of you. ~

APPLE CAKE

3 eggs
2 c. sugar
1 1/2 tsp. cinnamon
1/2 c. oil
1/2 tsp. salt

2 c. flour
2 tsp. soda
1 c. nuts, optional
4 c. apples, diced

Mix everything together except for apples. Stir in apples by hand. Put in a greased 9 x 13" pan. Spread topping on cake before baking. Bake at 325° for 1 hr.

TOPPING:

1 1/2 Tbsp. butter, melted
2 tsp. cinnamon
1/2 c. brown sugar

2 tsp. flour
1/2 c. chopped nuts, optional
1/4 c. raisins, optional

Mix together and pour over cake before baking.

Mrs. Margaret Yoder

APPLE NUT CAKE

1 1/4 c. oil
2 c. sugar
3 eggs
3 c. flour
1 tsp. salt

2 tsp. vanilla
1 c. nuts
1 tsp. soda
1 tsp. cinnamon
3 c. cubed apples

Mix all ingredients together, pour into a greased 9 x 13" pan and bake in a 350° oven. Start in a cold oven for 40 to 45 min.

TOPPING:

1/2 c. butter, 1/4 c. Carnation milk, 1 c. brown sugar.

Bring to a boil. Pour over cake while it is still warm.

MOIST CHOCOLATE CAKE

2 c. cake flour
1 tsp. salt
1 tsp. baking powder
2 tsp. soda
3/4 c. cocoa
2 c. sugar

1 c. vegetable oil
1 c. hot coffee
1 c. milk
2 eggs
1 tsp. vanilla

Sift together dry ingredients. Add oil, coffee, and milk. Mix. Add eggs and vanilla. Beat for 2 min. Bake at 350°.

Mrs. Nettie Miller

MOIST CHOCOLATE CAKE

Combine and cool:
1 c. boiling water, 2 tsp. soda.
Beat in:

2 1/2 c. brown sugar	**1 tsp. vanilla**
2 eggs	**1/2 c. cocoa**
3/4 c. vegetable oil	**1/2 tsp. salt**

Blend in alternately:
2 1/2 c. flour, and 1 c. sour milk or buttermilk.
Bake at 350° for 30 min.

Mrs. Sevilla Miller

PINEAPPLE UPSIDE DOWN CAKE

1 stick oleo	**maraschino cherries**
1 c. brown sugar	**yellow cake mix**
pineapple rings	

Melt oleo in a 9 x 13" oblong pan. Sprinkle sugar in oleo and stir gently. Arrange pineapples in bottom of pan. Place a cherry in middle of pineapple rings. Mix cake as directed on box and pour batter over pineapples. Bake at 350°. Flip out on a tray while still warm. Serve with ice cream.

Anna Yoder

PINEAPPLE NUT CAKE

2 c. flour	2 eggs
1 1/2 c. sugar	1 lg. can crushed
2 tsp. soda	pineapple and juice
1 tsp. salt	1/2 c. chopped nuts

Mix all ingredients together and pour into an ungreased 9 x 13 pan. Bake 35 to 40 min. at 350°. Remove from oven and cool for 15 min.

ICING:

8 oz. cream cheese	1/2 c. margarine
1 3/4 c. powdered sugar	chopped nuts
1 tsp. vanilla	

Mix ingredients together and sprinkle with nuts.

CARROT PINEAPPLE BUNDT CAKE

3 c. sifted cake flour
2 c. sugar
2 tsp. baking soda
1 tsp. salt
1 tsp. baking powder
2 tsp. ground cinnamon
3 eggs, slightly beaten
1 1/2 c. vegetable oil
2 tsp. vanilla
1 1/2 c. finely chopped walnuts
2 c. grated raw carrots
8 3/4 oz. can crushed pineapple with liquid

Sift flour, sugar, baking soda, salt, baking powder, and cinnamon together. Place in a large bowl. Drain pineapple and combine the liquid with eggs, oil and vanilla. Beat the egg mixture into the flour mixture on low speed until well mixed. Beat at medium speed for 3 min. Stir in pineapple, walnuts and carrots. Pour into a greased and floured bundt pan and bake in a preheated 325° oven for about 1 1/2 hours, or until toothpick inserted in cake comes out clean. Cool. Unmold onto plate. Spread with icing.

ICING:

1/4 c. butter, softened
2 (3 oz.) pkgs. cream cheese, softened
2 Tbsp. orange juice
1 tsp. vanilla
pinch of ground cinnamon
2 1/2 c. powdered sugar, approximately
1/4 c. chopped walnuts

Cream butter until light and fluffy. Beat in cream cheese, orange juice, vanilla and cinnamon. Continue beating while adding enough sugar for spreadable consistency. Stir in walnuts. Delicious and moist without icing.

Mrs. Ada Mullet

WHITE CAKE

1 1/2 c. sugar
1/2 c. butter
1 c. milk
1 tsp. vanilla in milk
3 c. flour
1/4 tsp. salt
3 heaping tsp. baking powder

Fold in whites of 5 eggs. Bake 23 to 25 min. in a 375° oven.

~ Kindness is the language the deaf can hear, and the blind can see. ~

WHITE CAKE

1 1/2 c. sugar
1/2 c. shortening
1 c. milk
3 egg whites
vanilla

2 1/2 c. flour
1/2 c. cornstarch
3 tsp. baking powder
pinch of salt

Cream shortening. Add sugar gradually and cream until fluffy. Sift together dry ingredients. Add to creamed mixture alternately with milk. Stir in flavoring, fold in egg whites, stiffly beaten. Bake at 350° for 25 to 30 min.

CARROT CAKE

2 c. sugar
1 1/2 c. Wesson oil
4 eggs
2 1/2 c. Gold Medal flour
1/2 c. chopped nuts

1 tsp. cinnamon
2 tsp. soda
1 tsp. salt
3 c. carrots, finely grated

Combine sugar and oil. Mix in eggs, beat until well mixed. Add flour, cinnamon, soda, and salt. Slowly mix in carrots and nuts. Bake at 300°.

ICING:

8 oz. sour cream
1 lb. powdered sugar
1/2 c. coconut

2 tsp. vanilla
1/4 lb. oleo

Mrs. (Junior) Edna Miller

CARROT CAKE

2 c. flour
2 c. sugar
2 tsp. cinnamon
1 tsp. salt

2 tsp. soda
4 eggs
3 c. carrots, grated

ICING:

8 oz. Philadelphia cream cheese
1 stick oleo
1 tsp. vanilla

1 c. chopped walnuts
1 box confectioners sugar

Cake: mix ingredients well. Bake at 350° in a 12 x 15" pan for 35 to 40 min. Spread icing on cooled cake.

Sarah Yoder

SUGAR N' SPICE CARROT CAKE

4 eggs	2 1/4 c. all-purpose flour
1 1/2 c. brown sugar	2 1/2 tsp. ground cinnamon
1 1/2 c. grated carrots	1 1/2 tsp. baking soda
1 1/3 c. vegetable oil	1 tsp. salt

Beat eggs and sugar until fluffy and slightly thick. Add carrots and oil. Blend well. Combine dry ingredients and stir into egg mixture. Pour into a greased 9 x 13 x 2" pan. Bake at 350° for 45 min. or until cake tests done.

FROSTING:

3 oz. cream cheese, softened	2 1/4 c. confectioner's sugar
1/4 c. butter or margarine, softened	1 tsp. grated orange peel

Combine cream cheese with butter. Gradually blend in sugar and orange peel.

LEMON - LIME REFRIGERATOR CAKE

3 oz. pkg. lime jello	1 pkg. lemon cake mix (Duncan Hines)

Dissolve jello in 3/4 c. boiling water. Add 1/2 c. cold water and set aside. Mix and bake cake as directed in a 9 x 13" pan. Cool cake 20 to 25 min. Poke deep holes in cake with fork. Pour jello mixture into holes. Refrigerate cake while preparing topping.

TOPPING:

2 1/2 c. whipped topping	1 1/2 c. cold milk
1 pkg. instant lemon pudding mix	

In a chilled bowl, blend ingredients until stiff. Frost cake. Keep refrigerated. Delicious!

Barbara Jean Mullet

~ No one is unemployed who minds his own business. ~

LEMON CAKE

1 box lemon cake mix	3/4 c. hot water
4 eggs	1 pkg. vanilla
3/4 c. oil	instant pudding
2 tsp. butter	2 c. powdered sugar
2 tsp. hot water	1/2 c. orange juice
	cool whip

Mix together cake mix, eggs, oil, 3/4 c. water and vanilla pudding until very smooth. Bake in a 9 x 13" pan at 350° for 25 min. While cake is warm punch holes all over top with wooden spoon. **Dressing:** Mix orange juice and powdered sugar. Pour hot water over soft batter. Mix together until smooth. Pour dressing over cake. Cool and serve with cool whip.

CARAMEL ICING

1/2 c. butter	1 c. brown sugar
1/4 c. milk	2 c. powdered sugar

Melt butter, add brown sugar on low heat, stirring constantly, about 4 min. Add milk, stir until mixture comes to a boil. Remove from heat. Slowly add powdered sugar, beating until smooth. Good on sweet rolls or creamsticks.

FLUFFY WHITE ICING

1/3 c. hot water	2 egg whites
1 c. sugar	1/4 tsp. cream of tartar

Cook sugar and water to a hard boil stage. Beat egg whites, add cream of tartar and keep beating until stiff. Gradually pour sugar mixture over egg whites. Keep whipping until cool or spreading consistency.

                                            Nora Yoder

WHITE CRISCO ICING

4 Tbsp. crisco	1 egg yolk
1/4 tsp. salt	1 tsp. vanilla
4 c. powdered sugar	6 to 8 Tbsp. milk, to
	right consistency

Mix together crisco, salt, egg yolk, and vanilla. Add powdered sugar and milk alternately. Cream until smooth.

CREAM CHEESE FROSTING

8 oz. cream cheese
1/4 c. butter or oleo
1 tsp. vanilla
1 lb. powdered sugar

Beat ingredients until smooth and fluffy.

BUTTER CREAM FROSTING

3/4 c. butter or oleo
3/4 c. milk or 1 c. cream
3 Tbsp. flour

Cook the above ingredients and cool. Mix together 1 1/2 tsp. vanilla, 1/2 c. butter or oleo and 3/4 c. white sugar. Add first part and beat together until fluffy.

COOL WHIP FROSTING

1 sm. pkg. instant pudding
1/4 c. powdered sugar
1 c. milk

Beat all ingredients together and add 8 oz. cool whip.

CREAMY CHOCOLATE FROSTING

3 Tbsp. butter, melted
3 1/2 c. powdered sugar
1/2 c. cocoa
1/3 c. milk
1 1/2 tsp. vanilla
salt

Add salt to sugar. Combine melted butter, and cocoa and add the milk and vanilla. Stir in the powdered sugar in 3 additions, beating until smooth each time. If too thin add more powdered sugar, if too thick add more milk.

STRAWBERRY FROSTING

3 Tbsp. butter or vegetable shortening
1/4 tsp. salt
2 1/2 c. confectioner's sugar
1/4 c. crushed strawberries
1 tsp. vanilla

Combine salt and shortening. Add sugar alternately with strawberries. Blend in vanilla. Frosting is good for angel food cake.

~ *A reckless driver is seldom reckless for very long.* ~

FLUFFY LEMON FROSTING

1 c. cold milk
1 pkg. (4 serving size) instant lemon pudding
1/4 c. powdered sugar
8 oz. cool whip

Combine milk, pudding mix and powdered sugar. Beat with wire whisk until smooth. Stir in cool whip.

My Favorite Recipes:

My Favorite Recipes:

Pies

PASTRY
(for a 9" double-crust pie)

2 1/4 c. flour   1/2 tsp. salt
2/3 c. shortening   1/3 c. cold water

Combine flour and salt in a mixing bowl. Cut shortening into flour with a pastry blender or two knives. (Do not overmix.) Blend only until particles are the size of peas. Add water one tablespoon at a time, sprinkling over mixture. Toss lightly with a fork until all particles of flour have been dampened. Use only enough water to hold the pastry together when it is pressed between two fingers. It should not feel wet. Roll dough into a round ball, handling as little as possible. Roll out on a lightly floured board into a circle 1/8" thick and 1" larger in diameter than the top of the pan. Put in pan and prick with a fork to prevent air bubbles. Bake at 450° for 12 to 15 min. or until golden brown. Cut slits in top dough to allow steam to escape while baking.

NEVER FAIL PIE DOUGH

2 c. flour   enough water to make a
dash of salt   nice dough
1 c. shortening

FILLING FOR RASPBERRY, BLACKBERRY, STRAWBERRY OR BLUEBERRY PIE
(9" double crust)

Mix **1 to 1 1/2 c. sugar** with **1/3 c. Gold Medal flour** and **1/2 teaspoon cinnamon.** Mix lightly through **4 c. of your choice fresh berries.** Pour into a pastry lined pie pan. Dot with **1 1/2 Tbsp. butter.** Cover with top crust. Cut slits through. Bake until crust is nicely browned and juice begins to bubble through slits in crust.
Temperature: 425°. Time: 35 to 40 min.
Note: For most filling use minimum amount of sugar, depending on the sweetness of berries.

~ *Practice makes perfect, so be careful what you practice.* ~

MINCE MEAT PIE FILLING
(to can)

Chop hamburger and fry or cook until tender or well done. To every cup of meat add the following:

3 c. apples, chopped	2 c. brown sugar
1 c. seeded raisins	1 tsp. ea. of cinnamon,
1 c. sweet cider	cloves and allspice

Combine all ingredients. Add water as needed, about 2 c. Simmer until apples are done. Put in cans and pressure cook about 90 min.

Mrs. (Junior) Edna Miller

PERFECT MERINGUE

1 Tbsp. cornstarch	3 egg whites
1 1/2 tsp. water	3 Tbsp. sugar
1/2 c. boiling water	1/8 tsp. salt

Mix cornstarch with 1 1/2 teaspoon water. Stir into 1/2 c. boiling water. Cook until thick and clear. Beat egg whites until stiff. Add sugar and salt. Add cooked cornstarch and beat until mixture stands in peaks. Spread on pie and brown at 375°.

PEACH PIE

9" 2 crust pastry	1/3 c. flour
5 c. sliced fresh peaches	1/4 c. cinnamon
1 tsp. lemon juice	3 Tbsp. butter
1 c. sugar	

Heat oven to 425°. Prepare pastry. Mix peaches and lemon juice. Stir together sugar, flour, and cinnamon; mix with peaches. Turn into pastry lined pie pan, dot with butter. Cover with top crust which has slits cut in it; seal and flute. Cover edge with aluminum foil to prevent excessive browning. Remove foil the last 15 min. of baking. Bake 35 to 45 min. or until crust is brown and juice begins to bubble through slits.

~ *If it goes in one ear and out the mouth - it's gossip.* ~

PEACH PIE

4 peaches
1/2 c. sugar
3/4 c. brown sugar
1/2 c. flour
1 Tbsp. butter
1 tsp. cinnamon
1 c. cream
unbaked pie shell

Mix together 1/2 c. sugar and peaches. (Sliced and peeled.) Let stand for 10 min. Combine brown sugar, flour, butter, and cinnamon. Sprinkle a layer over pie shell. Add peaches. Add cream to remaining crumbs and pour over peaches. Bake at 375° for 45 min.

PEACHY PEACH PIE

Combine and cook until thick:

1 c. sugar
1 c. 7-up
1 c. water
2 Tbsp. clear jel
2 tsp. light corn syrup

Stir in until dissolved:

3 oz. peach gelatin

Cool then fold in:

3 to 4 c. sliced peaches

Pour into a baked pie shell. Top with cool whip. This recipe can also be used with other fresh fruit and matching or complimenting fruit and gelatin flavors.

SOUR CREAM APPLE PIE

2 eggs
1 c. sour cream
1 c. sugar
6 Tbsp. all-purpose flour
1 tsp. vanilla
1/4 tsp. salt
3 c. chopped, peeled, cooking apples
1 unbaked pie shell (9")
3 Tbsp. melted butter
1/4 c. packed brown sugar

Beat eggs in a large bowl. Add sour cream. Stir in sugar, 2 Tbsp. flour, vanilla and salt, mixing well. Stir in apples. Pour into pie shell. Bake at 375° for 15 min. Meanwhile, combine butter, brown sugar and remaining flour. Sprinkle over top of pie. Return to oven for 20 to 25 min. or until filling is set. Cool completely. Serve or cover and refrigerate. Yield: 8 servings.

"GRANNY'S" APPLE PIE

Pastry for 9" double crust pie
6 large Granny Smith apples, pared, cored & sliced 1/4" thick
3/4 c. sugar
3/4 tsp. cinnamon
dash of salt
dash of nutmeg
2 Tbsp. butter
2 Tbsp. all-purpose flour

Place apples in a large bowl. Blend sugar, flour, cinnamon, nutmeg, and salt together and mix with sliced apples. Line a 9" pie plate with pastry dough and fill with apple mixture. Dot with butter. Adjust top crust and seal tightly. Brush melted butter over top crust, sprinkle with 1 Tbsp. of sugar. Cut 4 one inch slits in top to let steam escape. Bake in a preheated 400° oven for 1 hr. and 20 min.

SNITZ PIE

1/2 lb. snitz
3 Tbsp. cornstarch
2 c. brown sugar
1/4 tsp. salt
1 tsp. cinnamon

Soak snitz in water overnight. Cook on low heat until soft. Put through sieve. Add all ingredients plus enough applesauce to make 2 qts. Can be used to make half moon pies or regular snitz pie. Bake in hot oven.

DRIED APPLES (FOR SNITZ)

Peel, core and slice apples. Spread slices on cookie sheets. Put in oven at a very low temperature, 125° to 150° for 6 to 8 hours. Turn several times while drying. Pack in airtight containers and store in a cool dry place or in the freezer.

~ *Each one of us finds in others the very faults they find in us.* ~

HALF MOON PIES

1 gal. dried apple snitz
6 c. water or enough to cover snitz
2 c. sugar, or to taste
1 Tbsp. cinnamon, heaping
dash of allspice and cloves, optional
pie dough

Wash snitz. Place snitz in a large kettle with water. Cover and cook until snitz are soft and water is absorbed. Stir until smooth, using potato masher. Cool. When ready to use add sugar and spices. Shape pie dough to size of a large walnut and roll out to form a small circle. Mark half of dough with a pie crimper. Turn dough over and put 1 large tablespoon of filling on other half. Fold crimped half of dough over filling. Press edges together. Cut off remaining dough to make a neat edge. Brush top with a mixture of milk and a beaten egg. Sprinkle with sugar. Bake at 350° for 20 min. or until crust is baked.

GOLDEN APPLE BUNDLES

2 c. chopped, peeled apples
1/3 c. chopped walnuts
1/4 c. packed brown sugar
1/4 c. raisins
1 Tbsp. all-purpose flour
1/2 tsp. lemon peel
1/2 tsp. ground cinnamon
pastry for double pie crust
milk
sugar

In a bowl combine the apples, walnuts, brown sugar, raisins, flour, lemon peel and cinnamon. Set aside. Roll pastry to 1/8" thickness. Cut into 5" circles. Spoon about 1/4 c. of apple mixture into the center of each circle. Moisten edges of pastry with water. Fold over and seal edges with a fork. Place on a greased cookie sheet. Bake at 450° for 10 min. Reduce heat to 400°, bake 10 min. longer. Brush each with milk and sprinkle with sugar. Return to oven for 5 min. Yield: 10 to 12 servings.

~ It takes some folks a long time in telling you they have nothing to say. ~

IMPOSSIBLE CHERRY PIE

1 c. milk	1/2 c. bisquick baking mix
2 Tbsp. margarine or butter, softened	1/4 c. sugar
1/4 tsp. almond extract	21 oz. can cherry pie filling
2 eggs	streusel (below)

Heat oven to 400°. Grease pie plate, 10 x 1 1/2". Beat all ingredients (except for pie filling and streusel) until smooth. Pour into pie plate. Spoon pie filling on top. Bake for 25 min. Top with streusel. Bake until knife inserted in center comes out clean, about 10 min. longer.

STREUSEL: Cut 2 tablespoons margarine or butter into 1/2 c. bisquick mix, 1/2 c. packed brown sugar, and 1/2 teaspoon ground cinnamon until crumbly.

STRAWBERRY CHIFFON PIE

9" baked pie shell	3 egg whites
1/4 c. sugar	1/4 tsp. cream of tartar
1 env. flavored gelatin	1/3 c. sugar
1 pkg. (10 oz.) frozen strawberry halves, thawed	1/2 c. chilled whipping cream

Stir together 1/4 c. sugar and the gelatin in a saucepan. Stir in strawberries. Cook over medium heat, stirring constantly, just until mixture boils. Place pan in a bowl of ice and water or chill in refrigerator, stirring occasionally until mixture mounds slightly when dropped from spoon. Beat egg whites and cream of tartar until foamy. Beat in 1/3 c. sugar, 1 Tbsp. at a time, continue beating until stiff and glossy. Do not under beat. Fold strawberry mixture into meringue. In chilled bowl, beat cream until stiff, fold into strawberry meringue. Pile into baked pie shell. Chill at least 3 hours or until set.

STRAWBERRY PIE

2 c. sugar	3 Tbsp. cornstarch
2 c. water	3 oz. strawberry jello
3 Tbsp. flour	1 qt. sliced strawberries

Cook sugar, water, flour, and cornstarch until thick. Remove from heat. Add jello to cooked sugar and flour mixture. Add 1 Tbsp. butter, 1 Tbsp. vanilla, and a drop of almond flavoring. Pour mixture over berries. Pour into 2 baked pie crusts. Top with cool whip.

RAISIN PIE

3 oz. vanilla pudding mix
1 c. milk
1/2 c. water
1 c. raisins
1/2 tsp. vanilla extract
1 1/4 c. plain yogurt
whipped topping

In a saucepan combine (cook and serve) pudding mix, milk, and water. Cook over medium heat until thickened. Remove from heat. Stir in raisins and vanilla. Cool for 15 min. then stir in yogurt. Top with whipped topping.

Mrs. Anna Troyer

BLUEBERRY CREAM PIE

1 c. sour cream
2 Tbsp. flour
3/4 c. sugar
1 tsp. vanilla
1/4 tsp. salt
1 egg, beaten
2 1/2 c. fresh blueberries
1 unbaked 9" pastry shell
3 Tbsp. flour
1 1/2 Tbsp. butter
3 Tbsp. walnuts, chopped

Combine sour cream, flour, sugar, vanilla, salt, and egg. Beat 5 min. at medium speed or until smooth. Fold in blueberries. Pour into pastry shell. Bake at 400° for 25 min. Remove from oven and combine remaining ingredients, stirring well. Sprinkle over top of pie. Bake 10 more min. Chill. Yield: 8 servings.

HAPPINESS PIE

1 pt. blueberries
20 to 25 strawberries, hulled
cool whip
sm. pkg. vanilla pudding mix
2 c. milk
3 oz. cream cheese, softened
1/2 tsp. vanilla
8" prepared graham cracker crust

Combine pudding mix and milk in saucepan. Bring to a full boil over med. heat, stirring constantly. Remove from heat. Add cream cheese and stir until smooth. Add vanilla. Let mixture cool for 5 min., stirring twice. Pour pudding mixture into graham cracker crust. Refrigerate overnite or 3 hours. Place strawberries in a circle around edge of pie. Place one strawberry in center of pie. Place blueberries over remaining pudding surface. Serve with cool whip.

OATMEAL PIE

3 eggs, beaten
2/3 c. white sugar
1 c. brown sugar
2 tsp. oleo, softened
2/3 c. oatmeal
2/3 c. coconut
2/3 c. milk
1 tsp. vanilla

Blend together and bake in an unbaked pie shell for 30 to 35 min.

Mrs. Mabel Yoder

VANILLA CRUMB PIE

2 c. brown sugar
2 eggs, beaten
3 c. water
vanilla to flavor
1 1/2 c. white karo
1 c. flour
1/8 tsp. salt

Cook well and cool. Pour into unbaked pie shells.

CRUMBS:
2 c. flour
3/4 c. granulated sugar
3/4 tsp. soda
3/4 tsp. cream of tartar
1/2 c. shortening

Mix well, put on top of pie. Bake like custard. Yield: 2 pies.

Barbara Jean Mullet

SOUR CREAM RHUBARB PIE

3/4 c. white sugar
1/4 tsp. salt
1 egg, beaten
1/2 tsp. vanilla
2 Tbsp. flour
2 c. rhubarb, chopped
1 c. sour cream

Add all ingredients to beaten egg. Bake at 350° for 30 min. Top with the following crumbs, then bake 15 more min.

CRUMBS:
1/2 c. brown sugar *flour*
1/3 c. butter
3/4 c. butter

Alma Hershberger

RHUBARB PIE

Melt **2 Tbsp. butter.** Add **2 c. rhubarb.** Then add **1/2 c. water** and **1 c. sugar.** Cook slowly until tender. Combine **1/2 c. sugar, 2 Tbsp. cornstarch, 1/8 tsp. salt, 2 egg yolks, and 1/4 c. cream.** (Can substitute pet milk for cream if desired.) Cook until thick.

Barbara Troyer

PUMPKIN PIE

1/2 c. white sugar
1/2 c. brown sugar
1/2 tsp. pumpkin pie spice
2 c. milk
1/2 c. pumpkin
1 Tbsp. flour
1/2 tsp. salt
2 eggs, separated

Mix flour, sugar, spice, salt, and egg yolks together. Then add milk and beaten egg whites. Bake at 450° for 10 min. Reduce heat to 350° until done. Yield: 1 pie.

Linda Miller

DOUBLE LAYER PUMPKIN PIE

4 oz. cream cheese, softened
1 Tbsp. milk or half & half
1 Tbsp. sugar
1 1/2 c. cool whip
1 prepared graham cracker crust (6 oz.)
1 c. cold milk
2 (3 oz.) pkgs. vanilla instant pudding
16 oz. pumpkin
1 tsp. ground cinnamon
1/2 tsp. ground ginger
1/4 tsp. ground cloves

Mix cream cheese, 1 Tbsp. milk and sugar in a large bowl until smooth. Gently stir in whipped topping. Spread over crust. Pour 1 c. milk into bowl. Add pudding mixes. Beat with wire whisk for 1 min. Stir in pumpkin and spices until well mixed. Spread over cream cheese layer. Refrigerate 4 hours or until set. Garnish with additional whipped topping. Yield: 8 servings.

CUSTARD PIE

4 egg whites, beaten
2 Tbsp. flour
2 c. brown sugar
3 c. milk
1 can evaporated milk
salt

Mix flour, sugar and salt. Add milk, then add egg whites last. Bake at 400° for 10 min., finish at 350° for approximately 30 min.

Mrs. Sevilla Miller

CUSTARD PIE

1 c. brown sugar
1 Tbps. flour
3 eggs separated
3 c. milk
salt

Add beaten egg whites last. Yield: 1 pie.

Marie Kline

PECAN PIE

1/2 c. white sugar
2 Tbsp. butter, melted
1 1/4 c. white Karo
1 tsp. vanilla
pinch of salt
1/4 c. oats
1/2 c. nuts
3 eggs, beaten

Mix together first 6 ingredients, then add nuts and beaten eggs. Bake at 425° for 10 min. Reduce heat to 350° till done. Yield 1 pie.

Linda Miller

PECAN PIE

5 eggs
1 c. brown sugar
1 3/8 c. light Karo
2 1/2 Tbsp. flour (level)
1/2 c. cold water
2 1/2 Tbsp. butter, melted
1 1/2 c. pecans

Put nuts in an unbaked pie shell. Add mixture. Bake at 375° for 10 min., then 350° until done.

Mrs. Naomi Yoder

ABBY'S FAMOUS PECAN PIE

1 c. light Karo
1 c. brown sugar
3 eggs, slightly beaten
1/3 c. butter, melted
1/3 tsp. salt
1 tsp. vanilla
1 c. pecan halves or pieces
9" unbaked pie shell

Mix everything together except pecans. Sprinkle pecans on top before baking and bake at 350° for 40 to 45 min.

Anna Yoder

LEMON SPONGE PIE

1 c. granulated sugar
2 eggs, separated
juice of 1 lemon
2 Tbsp. flour
butter size of walnut
1 c. sweet milk

Cream butter and sugar. Add flour, lemon juice, milk, and egg yolks. Lastly fold in stiffly beaten egg whites. Pour into an unbaked pie shell and bake at 350° until firm.

Nora Yoder

~ *A person completely wrapped up in himself makes a small package.* ~

LEMON PIE

Juice of 1/2 lemon
3/4 c. cold water
2 egg yolks, beaten

1 c. sugar
1 pkg. lemon jello pie filling
1 3/4 c. boiling water

Add lemon juice to cold water. Mix sugar and pie filling and 1/2 of cold water mixture. Add egg yolks and remaining cold water mixture. Add boiling water. Boil and stir until thickened and clear. Pour into a 9" baked pie shell. Top with meringue.

LEMON MOCHA PIE

3/4 c. white sugar
1 1/4 c. milk
1/8 tsp. salt
1 pkg. gelatin

1/4 c. cold water
1 tsp. lemon jello
3/4 tsp. lemon flavoring
1 c. cool whip

Bring white sugar, milk, and salt to a boil. Remove from heat. Dissolve gelatin in cold water and add to hot mixture. Add lemon jello and flavoring. Cool till slightly thickened. Add cool whip to mixture. Add some yellow food coloring. Yield: 1 pie.

Iva Yoder

DUTCH CHOCOLATE PIE

1 .55 oz. milk chocolate
1 stick margarine
2 c. sugar
2 Tbsp. cornstarch
3 c. evaporated milk

2 eggs, separated
1 tsp. vanilla
pinch of salt
2 unbaked pie shells

In a large saucepan melt chocolate and margarine. Combine sugar, cornstarch, milk, egg yolks, vanilla, and salt. Stir in chocolate mixture. Beat egg whites and fold in last. Pour into pie shells. Bake at 450° for 12 min. and then at 350° until almost set. Cool and refrigerate. Serve with ice cream or cool whip. Yield: 2 pies.

~ After all, natures ways work sensibly, for the fatter you get, the farther you must sit from the table. ~

CREAMY CHOCOLATE LAYERED PIE

4 oz. cream cheese, softened
1 Tbsp. milk
1 Tbsp. sugar
12 oz. cool whip
6 oz. chocolate pie crust (Keebler Ready Crust)
1 1/2 c. cold milk
2 pkgs, instant chocolate pudding

Mix cream cheese, 1 Tbsp. milk and sugar in a large bowl until smooth. Stir in 1 1/2 c. of the whipped topping. Spread on crust. Pour milk into bowl and add pudding mixes. Beat with wire whisk. (Mixture will be thick.) Stir in 2 c. of the whipped topping. Spread over cream cheese layer. Refrigerate 4 hours or until set. Garnish with remaining cool whip. Yield: 8 servings.

CANDY BAR PIE

6 chocolate bars with almonds (1.45 oz. each
8 oz. cool whip
1 Tbsp. vanilla
1 graham cracker crust, prepared

In a double boiler melt chocolate bars. Quickly fold into the cool whip. Stir in vanilla. Spoon into the pie crust. Garnish with shaved chocolate if desired. Chill until ready to serve. Yield: 6 to 8 servings.

MALT BALL PIE

1 1/2 c. chocolate cookie crumbs
1/4 c. butter or oleo, melted
1 pt. softened vanilla ice cream
1/2 c. crushed malted milk balls
2 Tbsp. milk, divided
3 Tbsp. instant chocolate malted milk powder
3 Tbsp. marshmallow cream topping
1 c. whipping cream
additional whipped cream
additional malted milk balls

Combine crumbs and butter. Press into a 9" pie pan. Freeze while preparing filling. In a mixing bowl blend the ice cream, crushed malted milk balls and 1 Tbsp. milk. Spoon into crust and freeze for 1 hr. Meanwhile blend malted milk powder, marshmallow topping and remaining milk. Stir in whipping cream. Whip until soft peaks form. Spread over ice cream layer. Freeze overnite or several hrs. Garnish with whipped topping & malted milk balls before serving. Yield: 6 to 8 servings.

PEANUT BUTTER CREAM PIE

1 9" baked pie shell	1/3 c. creamy peanut butter
1 Tbps. butter	1/2 c. sugar
1/8 tsp. salt	2 1/2 c. milk
4 Tbsp. cornstarch	2 eggs, separated

Combine butter, sugar, milk, salt, cornstarch, peanut butter, and egg yolks. Cook in double boiler until thick. Cool and pour into baked pie shell.

TOPPING:
2 egg whites, beaten, 1/4 c. sugar, 1/2 tsp. vanilla.
Mix above ingredients and spread on pie. Brown in broiler if desired.

PEANUT BUTTER PIE

1/4 c. peanut butter   1/2 c. powdered sugar

Make crumbs and line the bottom of a baked pie shell. Save some for the top.

FILLING:

1/3 c. flour	2 Tbsp. butter
1/2 c. white sugar	1 tsp. vanilla
2 c. milk	1/8 tsp. salt
	3 egg yolks, slightly beaten

Mix everything except 1 c. milk. Heat the 1 c. milk, when hot, add the other mixture. Cook until thick, stirring constantly. Remove from heat and beat with electric mixer. Pour over crumbs in pie shell. Top with cool whip and sprinkle remaining crumbs on top.

PEANUT BUTTER PIE

8 oz. cream cheese, softened	1 lg. container cool whip
2 c. powdered sugar	graham cracker crust
1/2 c. peanut butter	

Cream cream cheese with powdered sugar. Add peanut butter and mix until smooth. Fold in cool whip. Place in pie pan with graham cracker crust. Chill for several hours. Garnish with whipped cream and the following crumbs:

1/4 c. peanut butter   1/2 c. powdered sugar

PEANUT BUTTER CUP PIE

1/2 c. sugar
1 Tbsp. flour
1 Tbsp. cocoa
1/4 c. milk
1 egg, beaten
1 1/2 tsp. vanilla

4 oz. cream cheese, softened
1/4 c. peanut butter
1/4 c. powdered sugar
1/2 tsp. vanilla
4 oz. cool whip

Combine the first 6 ingredients and pour into a pastry shell. Bake at 350° for around 20 min. or until set. Cool and chill. Next, mix other ingredients and spread over baked chocolate mixture. Put extra cool whip on top and sprinkle with grated chocolate. (I use chocolate chips.)

Iva Yoder

COCONUT CREAM PIE

1 1/2 c. milk
3/4 c. sugar
2 egg yolks, slightly beaten
1 Tbsp. unflavored gelatin
1 tsp. vanilla
2 egg whites

1/4 tsp. salt
1/2 c. whipped cream
1/2 c. toasted coconut
9" pastry crust

In a saucepan combine milk, 1/4 c. sugar and egg yolks. Cook over medium heat, stirring constantly until mixture coats a spoon. Do not boil. Pour 1/4 c. water in a bowl and sprinkle gelatin on top. Add to hot mixture and stir until dissolved. Add vanilla and salt. Chill mixture until slightly thickened. Beat egg whites and salt until foamy. Gradually add remaining sugar until stiff. Fold in gelatin mixture, whipped cream and coconut. Put in a pie shell and sprinkle coconut on top.

~ It there's not enough to save; but a little too much to dump, and you just can't help but eat it - Thats what makes the housewife plump. ~

MILLION DOLLAR PIE

2 baked 9" pastry shells
1/4 c. lemon juice
1 can eagle brand milk
1 c. chopped pecans
1 (2 lb.) can crushed
  pineapple, drained
9 oz. cool whip
flaked coconut

Stir lemon juice into milk until mixture thickens. Add pecans and pineapple, fold in cool whip. Pour 1/2 of mixture into each pie shell and sprinkle with coconut. Chill in refrigerator at least 2 hours.

KEY LIME PIE

9" graham cracker pie crust
1/2 c. fresh lime juice
1 tsp. grated rind
14 oz. sweet condensed milk
2 large egg yolks
1 c. heavy cream, whipped
  and sweetened with
1 Tbsp. powdered sugar

Refrigerate crust until cold. Mix lime juice and lime rind and gradually stir in milk until blended. Add egg yolks and beat until well blended. Pour lime mixture into crust and chill before serving. Top with whipped cream and serve. Yield: 6 to 8 servings.

RICE KRISPY PIE

2 eggs, beaten
2/3 c. white sugar
1/2 c. white Karo
1/4 tsp. salt
1 tsp. vanilla
3 Tbsp. melted butter
2 Tbsp. water

Fold in 1 c. rice krispies. Pour into an unbaked pie shell. Bake at 375° for 35 to 40 min.

Diane Keim

RICE KRISPIE PIE

2 c. rice krispies
1 Tbsp. butter or oleo, melted
1/2 c. marshmallow creme

Melt the butter and blend with marshmallow creme. Add rice krispies and mix. Place in a pie pan and shape like a crust. Fill crust with vanilla ice cream and freeze. Top with your favorite fruit when ready to serve.

~ *A word of advice - don't give it.* ~

CHONIE PIE

1 c. graham crackers, crushed
1 c. sugar
4 egg whites
1/2 c. nuts
1 tsp. vanilla
1/2 c. coconut

Beat egg whites and fold in last. Bake in a 9" pie pan. (No crust) Top with cool whip.

COOL 'N' EASY EASTER PIE

4 oz. jello (any flavor)
2/3 c. boiling water
whipped topping
8 oz. cool whip
1 graham cracker crust

Stir boiling water into gelatin until dissolved. Mix cold water and ice to make 1 1/4 c. Add to gelatin. When slightly thickened stir in whipped topping. Refrigerate 4 hours.

Mrs. Anna Troyer

FROZEN MINT PIE

6 oz. ready-made oreo pie crust
14 oz. can eagle brand sweetened condensed milk
1 to 1 1/2 tsp. peppermint extract
10 to 12 drops green food coloring
2 c. whipped topping

In a large mixing bowl, combine milk, peppermint, and food coloring. Fold in whipped topping. Place into crust. Cover and freeze until firm (about 6 hours). Garnish with chocolate curls, if desired. Yield: 1 pie.

~ *Even a mistake proves that at least you tried.* ~

My Favorite Recipes:

My Favorite Recipes:

Cookies

CHOCOLATE MINT BROWNIES

1 c. all-purpose flour	1 tsp. vanilla extract
1/2 c. butter or oleo, softened	16 oz. can chocolate flavored syrup
1/2 tsp. salt	
4 eggs	1 c. sugar

FILLING:

2 c. confectioner's sugar	1/2 tsp. mint extract
1/2 c. butter or margarine, softened	3 drops green food coloring
1 Tbsp. water	

TOPPING:

10 oz. mint chocolate chips	9 Tbsp. butter or margarine

Combine the first 7 ingredients in a large mixing bowl. Beat well. Pour into a greased 9 x 13 x 2" baking pan. Bake at 350° for 30 min. (Top of brownies will appear wet.) Cool. Combine filling ingredients. Beat until creamy. Spread over cooled brownies. Refrigerate until set. For topping, melt chocolate chips and butter in a double boiler. Cool to lukewarm, stirring occasionally. Spread over filling. Chill. Store in refrigerator. Yield: 5 to 6 doz.

ONE BOWL BROWNIES

4 sq. Baker's unsweetened chocolate	3 eggs
	1 tsp. vanilla
3/4 c. butter or oleo	1 c. flour
2 c. sugar	1 1/2 c. chopped nuts

Heat oven to 350°. Melt chocolate and oleo in double boiler. Stir sugar into chocolate until well blended. Mix in eggs and vanilla. Stir in flour and walnuts, mixing well. Spread in a greased 9 x 13" pan. Bake 30 to 35 min. or until toothpick inserted in center comes out with fudgy crumbs. Do not over bake. Cool. Cut into squares. Yield: 24 brownies.

CHOCOLATE MINT SUGAR COOKIES

2 1/2 c. all-purpose flour	2 eggs
1 1/2 tsp. baking powder	1 tsp. vanilla
3/4 tsp. salt	10 oz. pkg. Nestle's
1 1/4 c. sugar, divided	Toll House mint
3/4 c. vegetable oil	chocolate chips

Preheat oven to 350°. Combine flour, baking powder, and salt. Combine 1 c. sugar and vegetable oil. Beat in eggs and vanilla. Gradually add flour mixture. Stir in mint chocolate chips. Drop by rounded balls, rolled in remaining sugar on an ungreased cookie sheet. Yield: 5 1/2 doz. cookies.

CHOCOLATE NUT COOKIES

1 c. sugar	2 oz. unsweetened
1/2 c. shortening	chocolate, melted
2 eggs	2 c. bisquick baking mix
2 Tbsp. water	1 c. chopped nuts
1 tsp. vanilla	walnut or pecan halves
	Frosting (below)

Heat oven to 350°. Mix sugar, shortening, eggs, water, vanilla, and chocolate. Stir in bisquick mix and chopped nuts. Drop on ungreased cookie sheets, 2" apart. Bake until set, (about 15 min.) Cool. Frost with frosting.

QUICK CHOCOLATE FROSTING:
1 c. powdered sugar, 1/4 c. cocoa, and 2 to 3 Tbsp. water, until spreading consistency. Place pecan or walnut halves on frosting, on each cookie.

~ It's nice to be important, but its more important to be nice. ~

DOUBLE CHOCOLATE CRUNCH BARS

1/2 c. butter	1/2 c. nuts
3/4 c. sugar	2 Tbsp. cocoa
2 eggs	1/4 tsp. baking powder
1 tsp. vanilla	1/2 tsp. salt
3/4 c. flour	2 c. marshmallows

TOPPING:

6 oz. chocolate chips	1 1/2 c. Rice Krispies
1 c. peanut butter	

Cream butter and sugar. Beat in eggs and vanilla. Sift flour, cocoa, baking powder, and salt. Add nuts. Stir into egg mixture. Spead into a 9 x 13 x 2" baking pan. Bake at 350° for 15 to 20 min. Sprinkle miniature marshmallows evenly on top. Bake 3 min. Cool. In a double boiler melt chocolate chips and peanut butter. Add rice krispies. Spread over marshmallows. Chill & cut.

NO-BAKE CHOCOLATE OATMEAL COOKIES

2 c. white sugar	1/4 c. cocoa
1/2 c. milk	1/2 c. oleo
1/2 c. crunchy peanut butter	1 tsp. vanilla
3 c. quick oats	

Mix sugar, cocoa, milk, and oleo in a saucepan. Boil for 1 min. Remove from heat; stir in peanut butter, vanilla, and oatmeal. Drop on waxed paper. Let stand until firm.

OREO COOKIES

18 oz. cake mix (white or yellow)	2 Tbsp. cooking oil
	1/2 c. cocoa
2 eggs	2 Tbsp. water

Let stand 20 min. Do not refrigerate. Shape into balls. Flatten with bottom of a glass, greased, and into Nestle's Quick for each cookie. Bake about 8 min. at 300°.

FILLING:

1 envelope Knox gelatin	1 tsp. vanilla
1/4 c. cold water	1/2 c. crisco
1 Tbsp. plus 1 c. powdered sugar	

TRIPLE TREAT COOKIES

1 c. white sugar	1 c. brown sugar
1 c. oleo	1 c. peanut butter
2 eggs	2 tsp. soda
1 tsp. vanilla	1 1/2 tsp. salt
3 c. flour	1 1/2 c. chocolate chips

Combine ingredients and roll dough into balls. Bake at 350°. Combine filling ingredients and put between 2 cookies.

FILLING:

1/2 c. peanut butter	1 tsp. vanilla
1/3 c. milk	3 c. powdered sugar

Mrs. Naomi Yoder, Mrs. Nettie Miller

EVERYTHING COOKIES

1 c. brown sugar	1 c. white sugar
1/2 c. oleo	2 eggs, beaten
1 tsp. cream of tartar	1 c. oatmeal
1/2 c. salad oil	2 Tbsp. vanilla
1 tsp. salt	1 tsp. baking powder
3 c. flour	1 c. Crispy Rice cereal
1 c. chocolate chips or M & M's	

Drop by teaspoonful on baking sheet. Bake at 350° for 10 to 12 min.

Mrs. Lizzie Keim, Mrs. Ida Miller

POTATO CHIP COOKIES

1 c. shortening	1 c. white sugar
1 c. chopped nuts	1 c. brown sugar
2 c. flour	1 tsp. baking soda
2 eggs	1 tsp. vanilla
2 c. crushed potato chips	

Mix together shortening, sugars, flour, soda, vanilla, and eggs. Add chips and nuts. Shape into balls. Place on cookie sheets, press with fork. Bake at 350° for 10 min.

~ Its not so much the bonnet but the head thats in it, thats what counts. ~

JELLO COOKIES

2 1/4 c. flour
1 tsp. soda
1/2 c. butter
1/2 tsp. almond flavoring
1 tsp. vanilla
1/2 tsp. salt
1/2 c. milk
1/2 c. sugar
2 eggs
3 oz. pkg. jello, any flavor

Cream sugar, jello, butter, salt, and eggs. Add flavoring and milk, then flour and soda. Drop on ungreased cookie sheets. Bake at 350°. They are good with powdered sugar frosting with the same flavor as the cookies.

CHOCOLATE MARSHMALLOW COOKIES

1 3/4 c. flour
1/2 tsp. soda
1/2 tsp. salt
1/4 c. cocoa
1/2 c. shortening
1 egg
1 c. sugar
1/2 c. milk
1/2 c. chopped nuts, optional
1 tsp. vanilla
marshmallows, cut in half

Sift flour with soda, salt, and cocoa. Cream shortening. Add sugar gradually, blending well. Add egg and beat well. Add flour mixture and milk alternately, beating well each time. Blend in vanilla and nuts. Drop on cookie sheets and bake at 350° for 8 min. Top with half of a marshmallow. Bake until marshmallow is soft. Cool and frost.

FROSTING:

1/3 c. oleo
1 c. brown sugar
2 tsp. cocoa
1/4 c. milk

Boil until it bubbles. Cool and add powdered sugar till right consistency.

Nora Yoder

~ When it comes to giving most people have short arms and deep pockets. ~

DEBBIE COOKIES

Cream:
1 c. oleo   3 c. brown sugar
Add:
4 eggs   2 Tbsp. vanilla
Blend in:
2 c. all-purpose flour   2 tsp. cinnamon
1 tsp. salt   1/2 tsp. nutmeg
1 1/2 tsp. baking powder
Add:
3 c. oatmeal

Drop on ungreased cookie sheet. Bake at 350°. Do not overbake.

FILLING:
Beat 2 egg whites till stiff. Gradually add 3 c. powdered sugar. Blend in until smooth and creamy. Add 1 Tbsp. vanilla and 1 c. softened shortening.

DEBBIE COOKIES

4 1/2 c. brown sugar   3/4 tsp. nutmeg
2 c. oleo   3 tsp. vanilla
6 eggs   3 c. flour
1 1/2 tsp. salt   6 c. oats
2 1/4 tsp. soda   2 c. chocolate chips
3 tsp. cinnamon

Mix well and bake at 350°. Spread filling between 2 cookies.

FILLING:
3 egg whites   3 c. powdered sugar
1/2 Tbsp. vanilla   1 1/2 c. shortening

Beat egg whites, add vanilla and powdered sugar. Beat in shortening.

Linda Miller

~ Some people are like eggs, too full of themselves to hold any thing else. ~

PEANUT BUTTER FINGERS

1 c. white sugar	2 eggs
1 c. brown sugar	2 tsp. salt
1 c. shortening	1 tsp. vanilla
2 c. flour	1 tsp. soda
2 c. oatmeal	3/4 c. peanut butter

Bake at 350°. When done put 1 c. chocolate chips on top. Let set 5 min. Spread with knife. Mix 2 c. powdered sugar, 1/2 c. peanut butter and 2 to 4 Tbsp. milk. Spread over chips then cut into squares.

Barb Byler

IRRESISTABLE PEANUT BUTTER COOKIES

3/4 c. peanut butter	1 egg
1/2 c. crisco	1 3/4 c. all-purpose flour
1 1/4 c. brown sugar	3/4 tsp. salt
3 Tbsp. milk	3/4 tsp. baking soda
1 Tbsp. vanilla	

Heat oven to 375°. Combine peanut butter, crisco, sugar, milk, and vanilla. Beat well. Add egg. Combine flour, baking soda, and salt. Add to creamed mixture. Drop by teaspoonful on ungreased cookie sheet. Flatten slightly with prongs of fork in a crisscross pattern. Bake for 7 to 8 min. or until set and beginning to brown. Yield: 3 dozen cookies. Variation: Shape into 1 1/2" balls and press center with teaspoon. Bake 7 to 8 min. Press mini peanut butter cup into depression. Roll into chopped peanuts first, if desired.

PEANUT BUTTER OATMEAL COOKIES

3/4 c. butter flavor crisco	1 tsp. vanilla
1 c. peanut butter	3 c. quaker quick oats
1 1/2 c. brown sugar	1 1/2 c. all-purpose flour
1/2 c. water	1/2 tsp. baking soda
1 egg	granulated sugar

Beat first 3 ingredients until creamy. Beat in water, egg and vanilla. Add combined dry ingredients; mix well. Cover. Chill for about 2 hours. Shape into 1" balls and place on ungreased cookie sheet. Flatten with tines of fork dipped in granulated sugar to form a crisscross pattern. Bake at 350° for 9 to 11 min. Cool 1 min. on cookie sheet before removing.

OATMEAL COOKIES

2 c. brown sugar
1 c. butter
2 eggs
2 tsp. soda
2 tsp. baking powder
1/2 tsp. salt
1 tsp. vanilla
2 c. flour
2 c. oatmeal
1/2 c. coconut
2/3 c. chocolate chips
1 c. M & M's

Mix well and bake at 350°.

Linda Miller

FORGOTTEN COOKIES

Preheat oven to 350°.

In a mixing bowl place:

2 egg whites.

Beat at high speed until soft peaks form. Slowly add and beat until stiff:

3/4 c. sugar

Fold in:

6 oz. pkg. semi-sweet chocolate chips

Drop by teaspoonful onto two greased cookie sheets. Place in oven then turn off heat. Let remain in oven until room temperature. Store in airtight containers.

TWINKIES

1 box yellow cake mix
1 pkg. instant pudding, any flavor
4 eggs
3/4 c. water
3/4 c. oil

Mix and bake at 350°. When cool slice in half and put the following filling between the 2 cakes.

FILLING:

1/2 c. crisco
1 c. marshmallow creme
3 to 4 tsp. milk
2 c. powdered sugar
1 tsp. vanilla

Ruby Beachy

~ What you're doing is not work unless you would rather be doing something else. ~

APPLE CHEESE BARS

CRUST:
1/2 c. granulated sugar
1 c. butter, softened
2 eggs, separated
1 tsp. baking powder
1/2 tsp. salt
2 c. all-purpose flour
  (can be part rolled oats)

FILLING:
4 cooking apples,
  (about 4 c. grated)
8 oz. grated cheddar cheese
1/4 c. flour
3/4 c. granulated sugar
1 tsp. ground cinnamon

TOPPING:
reserved egg whites
1/4 c. cream cheese, softened
1 1/2 c. confectioner's sugar

For crust combine all ingredients until crumbly, using egg yolks. Press 1/2 of mixture in a 9 x 13" pan. Set other half aside. Grate apples and cheese together in one bowl. Add other filling ingredients. Mix well and spread over crust. Spread remaining crumbs over filling. For topping, whip egg whites until peaks form. Gradually add cream cheese and sugar, beating constantly. Spoon evenly over all layers. Bake at 350° for 30 to 35 min., or until light brown. Yield: 36 bars.

CHOCOLATE CARAMEL BARS

1 pkg. (50) caramels
1/3 c. evaporated milk

Combine and cook over low heat until caramels are melted.

1 pkg. german chocolate
  cake mix
3/4 c. butter, melted
1 c. nuts
1 c. chocolate chips
1/3 c. evaporated milk

Combine dry cake mix, butter, evaporated milk and nuts. By hand, stir until dough holds together. Press half of dough into a greased 9 x 13" pan. Bake at 350° for 6 min. Sprinkle chocolate chips over baked crust. Spread caramel mixture over chocolate chips. Crumble rest of dough over caramel mixture. Return to oven for 15 to 18 min. longer. Cool and cut into squares.

Ruth Ann Troyer

~ A smooth tongue often hides sharp teeth. ~

PEANUT BUTTER CHOCOLATE BARS

1 c. peanut butter	1 tsp. vanilla extract
6 Tbsp. butter, softened	3 eggs
1/2 c. white sugar	1 c. all-purpose flour
3/4 c. brown sugar	2 c. Nestles Toll House morsels, divided

Mix together peanut butter, sugars, vanilla, and butter in a large bowl until creamy. Beat in eggs and flour. Stir in 3/4 c. of morsels. Spread into a 9 x 13" pan. Bake in preheated oven at 350° for 20 to 25 min. or till edges are lightly browned. Remove from oven. Immediately sprinkle with remaining morsels. Let stand for 5 min. Spread. Sprinkle colored sugar over melted chocolate if desired.

FUDGE-NUT BARS

2 c. butter or oleo	4 c. brown sugar
4 eggs	4 tsp. vanilla
5 c. flour	2 tsp. soda
6 c. quick oats	2 tsp. salt

Cream together butter and sugar. Mix in eggs and vanilla. Sift together dry ingredients, add to creamed mixture. Spread a thin layer of oatmeal mixture in a greased pan saving about 1/4 of mixture for top. Cook filling and spread over oatmeal mixture in pan. Dot with remainder of oatmeal mixture. Bake at 350° for 25 to 30 min. Do not over bake.

FUDGE-NUT FILLING:

12 oz. chocolate chips	1 can eagle brand milk
2 Tbsp. oleo	1/2 tsp. salt
1 c. chopped nuts	2 tsp. vanilla

In double boiler melt milk, chips, oleo, and salt. Stir in nuts and vanilla.

Laura Miller, Barbara Jean Mullet

~ Advice is like cooking - you should try it before you feed it to others. ~

DELICIOUS BARS
CRUMBS:

2 c. brown sugar   1/2 c. soft oleo
2 c. flour

Reserve 1 c. crumbs for top. Add the following to the rest of crumbs.

1 egg, beaten   1 tsp. salt
1 c. milk   1 tsp. soda
1 tsp. vanilla

Spread in a 9 x 13" pan. Sprinkle the following ingredients on top.

3/4 c. chocolate chips   1 c. crumbs
1/2 c. nuts

Bake at 350° for 20 to 25 min.

                                        Mrs. Lizzie Keim

LEMON BARS

1 c. butter   1/2 c. powdered sugar
2 c. flour

Mix above ingredients like pie dough and add a pinch of salt. Pat into a 9 x 13" pan. Bake at 350° for 15 to 20 min. (Barely brown.)

4 eggs, beaten   2 c. white sugar
4 Tbsp. flour   6 Tbsp. lemon juice

Beat above ingredients together and pour over baked crust. Bake at 350° for 20 to 30 min. Do not overbake.

                                        Barbara Jean Mullet

EASY LEMON COOKIES

1 box lemon cake mix   2 c. cool whip
1 egg

Beat together and refrigerate 2 hours. Make dough into small balls and roll into powdered sugar. Put on cookie sheet and flatten with the bottom of a glass. Bake at 350° until set.

                                        Barbara Jean Mullet

~ We may give without loving, but we cannot love without giving. ~

BUTTERMILK CHOCOLATE BARS

1 c. butter	2 eggs
1 c. water	1 tsp. soda
1/4 c. cocoa	1 tsp. vanilla
1/2 c. milk	1/2 tsp. salt
1 tsp. vinegar	2 1/4 c. flour
2 c. sugar	

Cook together butter, water, and cocoa. Cool. Add vinegar to milk. Add to cooled mixture. Add rest of ingredients. Bake at 350° for 25 min.

FROSTING:

1/2 c. butter	3 1/2 c. powdered sugar
1/4 c. cocoa	nuts
1/4 c. milk	

Melt butter then stir in rest of ingredients. Spread on bars while still warm.

Linda Miller

OH HENRY BARS

4 c. quick oatmeal	1/2 c. white sugar
1 c. brown sugar	1/2 c. oleo

Press in loaf pan and bake at 350° for 15 to 20 min.

TOPPING:

Melt 1/4 c. cocoa with 1 Tbsp. crisco and 2 Tbsp. oleo. Stir in 3 Tbsp. hot water and powdered sugar until thick enough to spread. Then stir in 3/4 c. peanut butter. Spread on cooled, baked layer.

Barbara Jean Mullet

REESE'S CHEWY CHOCOLATE PAN COOKIES

1 1/4 c. butter or oleo, softened	3/4 c. Hershey's cocoa
2 c. sugar	1 tsp. baking soda
2 eggs	1/2 tsp. salt
2 tsp. vanilla	2 c. Reese's peanut butter chips
2 c. all-purpose flour	

Heat oven to 350°. Grease a 15 1/2 by 10 1/2" jelly roll pan. In a large bowl, beat butter and sugar until light and fluffy. Add eggs and vanilla, beat well. Combine flour, cocoa, baking soda, and salt. Gradually blend into creamed mixture. Stir in chips. Spread batter into prepared pan; bake 20 min. or until set. Cool completely. Cut into bars.

Diane Keim

SEVEN-LAYER BARS

1/2 c. butter or margarine
1/2 c. graham crackers, crushed
6 oz. pkg. chocolate chips
1 c. nuts, optional
1 1/3 c. coconut
6 oz. pkg. butterscotch pieces
14 oz. can sweet condensed milk

Melt butter. Stir in graham crackers. Pat crumb mixture evenly in bottom of an ungreased 9 x 13" pan. Layer in order of: chocolate chips, butterscotch pieces, nuts, and coconut. Pour milk on top. Bake at 350° for 30 min. Cool. Cut into squares.

Karen Raber

REBEL BARS

1 c. oleo, softened
2 c. brown sugar
3 c. rolled oats
2 1/2 c. flour
2 eggs
1 tsp. soda
pinch of salt
2 tsp. vanilla

Put 2/3 of dough into a pan. Melt together the following ingredients and spread on top. Put remaining dough on top of the following mixture in chunks.

1 can eagle brand milk
1 tsp. vanilla
12 oz. chocolate chips

SURPRISE BARS

1 1/2 c. cooking oil
2 c. sugar
4 eggs
2 c. sifted flour
2 tsp. baking soda
1 c. nuts
1 c. raisins
2 tsp. cinnamon
3 c. carrots, grated

Cream sugar and oil together, add eggs, beating well. Sift dry ingredients and add to egg mixture. Fold in carrots, nuts and raisins. Pour into a greased and floured, 4 sided, 10 x 15" cookie pan. Bake at 350° for 40 min. Frost when cool.

FROSTING:
3 1/2 c. powdered sugar
1 Tbsp. milk
3 oz. cream cheese, softened
1 tsp. vanilla
6 Tbsp. oleo or butter

Mrs. Ada Mullet

MARBLE SQUARES

1/2 c. oleo	1 c. plus 2 Tbsp. flour
1/2 c. sugar, scant	1/2 tsp. soda
1/2 c. brown sugar	1/2 tsp. salt
1 1/2 tsp. vanilla	1/2 c. nuts, chopped
1 tsp. water	(optional)
1 egg	1 c. chocolate chips

Blend oleo, sugars, vanilla and water until creamy. Beat in egg. Sift and add flour, soda and salt. Add nuts. Spread in a 9" square pan or med. sized loaf pan that has been greased. Sprinkle with chocolate chips. Bake at 375° for 3 min. Run a knife through to marbilize; return to oven and bake 12 to 14 min. longer. Do not overbake or they will be hard.

Mrs. Margaret Yoder

CREAM CHEESE BARS

16 oz. cream cheese   2 cans crescent rolls

Place 1 can crescent rolls on a 9 x 13" cookie sheet. Mix cream cheese at room temperature with 1/2 c. sugar and 1 tsp. vanilla. Spread over crescent rolls. Put other can crescent rolls on top. Mix 1/2 c. sugar and 1 Tbsp. cinnamon. Sprinkle over top. Melt 1/4 c. butter. Pour over cinnamon mixture. Bake at 350° for 30 to 35 min.

RASPBERRY BARS

3/4 c. margarine	1/2 tsp. soda
1 c. brown sugar	1 1/2 c. quick oats
1 1/2 c. flour	10 oz. jar Kraft raspberry
1 tsp. salt	preserves

Cream margarine and sugar until light and fluffy. Combine dry ingredients and add to sugar and margarine mixture, mixing well. Press 1/2 of mixture into a greased 9 x 13" baking pan. Spread with preserves and sprinkle remaining mixture over preserves. Bake at 400° for 20 to 25 min.

BUTTERSCOTCH COOKIES

3 1/2 c. brown sugar	1 Tbsp. soda
1 c. butter or lard mixed	1 Tbsp. vanilla
4 eggs	1 Tbsp. cream of tartar
3/4 c. cold water	1 tsp. salt
	7 c. flour

Form into a roll. Chill, slice and bake at 350°.

BUTTERSCOTCH DROP COOKIES

2/3 c. butter or oleo
1 1/2 c. brown sugar
2 eggs
1 tsp. vanilla
1 c. chopped nuts
1 c. evaporated milk
1 Tbsp. vinegar
1 tsp. soda
1/2 tsp. baking powder
1/2 tsp. salt
1 pkg. butterscotch chips
1 c. oatmeal
2 1/2 c. flour

Cream butter and brown sugar until light. Add eggs. Beat well. Add vanilla and vinegar to milk. Sift dry ingredients and add alternately with milk to creamed mixture. Stir in nuts, chips and oatmeal. Drop by spoonfuls on greased cookie sheet. Bake at 350° for around 15 min. Cool and frost.

FROSTING:

Melt 1/4 c. butter and add 1 c. brown sugar. Boil over low heat 2 min., stirring constantly. Add 1/4 c. milk and stir until mixture boils well. Cool to lukewarm. Add 1/4 tsp. vanilla and 2 c. powdered sugar. Beat until smooth. Add more powdered sugar if needed.

Ruth Ann Miller

WHITE CHOCOLATE COOKIES

1/2 c. butter or margarine
1 1/2 c. shortening
2 1/4 c. sugar
1 1/2 c. brown sugar
3 eggs
6 1/2 c. flour
3 tsp. baking soda
1 1/2 tsp. salt
2 tsp. vanilla
4 tsp. water
* 30 oz. white chocolate, finely chopped
* 1 c. toasted macadonia nuts, coarsely chopped

Cream butter and shortening. Add sugars, beating till light and fluffy. Add eggs, mixing well. Combine flour, soda, and salt, add to creamed mixture. Blend in vanilla and water. Stir in chocolate and nuts. Drop by teaspoonful onto ungreased cookie sheet. Bake at 350° for 12 to 15 min. or until lightly browned. Let stand a few minutes before removing to cool. * Chocolate chips can be used instead of white chocolate and macodonia nuts can be substituted for English walnuts.

Mary Beth Troyer

COFFEE CAKE COOKIES

1 pkg. dry yeast	4 c. flour
1/4 c. lukewarm water	1 c. milk
1 tsp. salt	2 eggs, beaten
1 c. crisco	1 c. sugar
1/4 c. sugar	1 tsp. cinnamon

Put flour, salt and 1/4 c. sugar in a bowl. Cut in shortening. Dissolve yeast in warm water. Scald milk and cool. Combine eggs with milk and add yeast. Add liquid to flour, mix lightly till flour is moist. Do not knead. Refrigerate overnite. Divide dough in half. Roll out like cinnamon rolls. Mix 1 c. sugar and 1 tsp. cinnamon. Sprinkle on rolled out dough. Roll up and cut in 5/8" slices. Place on cookie sheets. Bake at 350° for 10 min.

ICING:

4 Tbsp. butter	1 tsp. vanilla
1 1/2 c. powdered sugar	

Melt and brown butter. Add vanilla and powdered sugar. Blend with hot water till spreading consistency.

Ruth Ann Troyer

PEANUT BUTTER BLOSSOMS

3 1/2 c. flour	1 c. peanut butter
1 c. white sugar	4 tsp. milk
1 c. shortening	2 eggs, lightly beaten
1 tsp. salt	2 tsp. vanilla
2 tsp. soda	48 chocolate kisses
1 c. brown sugar	(Hershey's)

Cream shortening, sugars, and beaten eggs. Add remaining ingredients. Top each cookie with a candy kiss immediately when removed from oven. Press down firmly so cookie cracks around edge.

Mrs. Ada Mullet

~ *Friends are the sunshine of life.* ~

SPELL BINDERS

3 c. flour
1 tsp. baking powder
2 eggs
2 c. cornflakes, crushed
1 1/2 c. oleo
2 c. brown sugar
2 c. quick oats

Make dough into balls and roll in cornflakes.

ICING:
4 Tbsp. oleo
2 c. powdered sugar
2 Tbsp. hot water
2 tsp. vanilla

Dribble on cooled cookies.

Susie Yoder

CREAM WAFERS

1 c. brown sugar
1/2 c. oleo
2 eggs, beaten
1 tsp. vanilla
1 tsp. soda
2 3/4 c. flour
2 Tbsp. milk

FILLING:
1/2 c. butter, melted
1 c. brown sugar

Stir together and boil over low heat for 2 min. Add 1/4 c. milk and bring to a boil stirring constantly. Cool to lukewarm. Add powdered sugar to right consistency. Put filling between 2 cookies. Use cookie press or drop.

Barbara Jean Mullet

MAPLE LEAF COOKIES

1 lb. oleo or butter
4 c. brown sugar
8 eggs
12 Tbsp. Rich's topping
10 c. flour
1 tsp. salt
6 tsp. soda
4 Tbsp. maple flavoring

Mix in order given. Roll out and cut, any design cutter. Bake at 350° for 10 to 12 min. Do not overbake.

FILLING:
2 egg whites, beaten
1 Tbsp. vanilla
1 Tbsp. flour
2 c. powdered sugar
1 tsp. cream of tartar

Mix and beat well. Add 1/2 c. crisco and 3/4 c. marshmallow topping. Cream until smooth. Spread filling between 2 cookies.

SOFT SUGAR COOKIES

2 c. white sugar
1 c. oleo
2 eggs
5 c. flour
2 tsp. baking powder
2 tsp. soda
1/2 tsp. salt
1 tsp. vanilla
1 c. buttermilk

Cream sugar, oleo, and eggs together. Add flour and rest of ingredients with buttermilk. Mix together.

ICING:
6 Tbsp. oleo, melted
1 tsp. vanilla
Powdered sugar and milk until spreading consistency

Mrs. Martha Schlabach

BEST SUGAR COOKIES UNDER HEAVEN

4 c. flour
1 tsp. salt
1 tsp. baking soda
1 tsp. cream of tartar
1 c. butter or oleo
1 c. salad oil
1 c. confectioner's sugar
1 c. granulated sugar
2 eggs
1 tsp. vanilla

Combine first 4 ingredients. Set aside. Cream butter, salad oil, and both sugars together. Add eggs and vanilla. Continue beating. Gradually add dry ingredients until combined. Wrap and refrigerate for 1 hour. Roll into balls and press down with bottom of a glass. Roll in sugar. Bake at 350°.

DATE FILLED COOKIES

1 c. white sugar
2 eggs, beaten
6 1/2 to 7 c. flour
4 tsp. baking powder
1 c. brown sugar
1 c. milk
1 c. shortening
2 tsp. soda

Cream shortening and sugar. Add eggs, milk, baking powder, soda, and enough flour to make a soft dough. Chill and roll thin, then cut. Use any design cutter. Put filling between 2 cookies. Bake at 375° till golden brown. Use 1 tsp. filling to each cookie.

FILLING:
Grind: 1/2 lb. dates
1 c. sugar
1 c. water
2 Tbsp. flour

Cook till thick, then chill. You can also add chopped walnuts or pecans to filling before it cools.

BUTTERMILK COOKIES

4 c. brown sugar
2 c. shortening
3 eggs
2 c. buttermilk
salt

2 tsp. soda
2 tsp. baking powder
1 tsp. nutmeg
1 tsp. ginger

Add enough flour to make a soft dough.

Mrs. Sevilla Miller

MONSTER COOKIES

6 eggs
2 c. brown sugar
2 c. white sugar
2 sticks oleo
2 1/2 c. peanut butter

4 tsp. soda
9 c. oatmeal
8 oz. chocolate chips
8 oz. M & M's

Mrs. Mabel Yoder

MONSTER COOKIES

1/2 c. butter
1 1/4 c. brown sugar
1 c. sugar
3 eggs
1 1/2 c. peanut butter

2 tsp. baking soda
4 1/2 c. rolled oats
1/2 c. chocolate chips
2 tsp. vanilla
1/2 c. M & M's

Combine and mix the first 4 ingredients. Add remaining ingredients. Bake at 350° for 10 min.

PARTY M & M COOKIES

1 c. oil or butter
2 c. brown sugar
1 c. white sugar
4 tsp. vanilla
4 eggs, beaten

6 c. flour
2 tsp. soda
2 tsp. salt
3/4 c. plain M & M's

Mix sugar, butter, eggs, and vanilla. Add salt and soda. Add flour and mix well. Add M & M's last. Bake at 350°.

Elmina Beachy

CHOCOLATE PIXIES

1/2 c. oleo
1/2 c. cocoa
4 eggs
2 c. white sugar
3 c. all-purpose flour
2 tsp. baking powder
1/2 tsp. salt
1/2 c. chopped nuts (optional)

Melt oleo and cocoa over low heat and set aside. Beat eggs and sugar. Add cocoa mixture. Sift flour, baking powder, and salt. Add to egg mixture and stir in walnuts. Chill dough 30 min. Roll into balls and roll these in powdered sugar. Bake at 300° for 15 to 18 min. They will have a crinkle top.

Mrs. Mary Ellen Wengerd

WHOOPIE COOKIES

4 c. flour
2 c. sugar
2 tsp. soda
1/2 tsp. salt
1 c. shortening
FILLING:
2 egg whites, beaten
1 Tbsp. vanilla
1 c. cocoa
2 eggs
2 tsp. vanilla
1 c. thick sour milk
1 c. cold water

2 c. confectioner's sugar
1 1/2 c. crisco

Beat first 3 ingredients well then add crisco and continue beating until smooth. Spread between 2 cookies.

Mrs. Wilma Hochstetler

WHOOPIE PIES

1 c. shortening
1/2 tsp. salt
2 tsp. soda
2 c. sugar
4 c. flour
1 c. cocoa
2 eggs
2 tsp. vanilla
1 c. thick sour milk
1 c. cold water

Cream together sugar, salt, shortening, vanilla, and eggs. Sift together flour, soda, and cocoa. Add milk and water to creamed mixture then mix altogether. Add slightly more flour if milk is not thick enough. Drop on cookie sheets and bake at 350°.

FILLING:
3 egg whites
3 tsp. vanilla
3 c. powdered sugar
1 1/2 c. crisco
6 tsp. milk

Beat egg whites until stiff. Add vanilla, milk, and powdered sugar, then crisco. Put filling between 2 cookies.

Nancy Miller

PUMPKIN WHOOPIE PIE COOKIES

- 2 c. brown sugar
- 1 c. vegetable oil
- 1 1/2 c. pumpkin
- 2 eggs, beaten
- 1 tsp. soda
- 1 tsp. vanilla
- 1/2 tsp. cloves
- 1/2 tsp. ginger
- 1 1/2 tsp. cinnamon
- 1 tsp. salt
- 1 tsp. baking soda
- 3 c. flour

Mix in order given. Bake at 350°. Put filling between 2 cookies when cool.

FILLING:
- 2 c. powdered sugar
- 1 c. marshmallow creme
- 1/2 c. crisco
- vanilla

Susie Yoder

PUMPKIN BARS

- 4 eggs, beaten
- 1 c. salad oil
- 1 c. pumpkin
- 2 c. sugar
- 1/2 tsp. salt
- 2 tsp. baking powder
- 1 tsp. soda
- 2 c. flour
- 1 c. nuts, optional

Combine all dry ingredients in a bowl. Cream eggs, oil and pumpkin in a separate bowl, then add dry ingredients. Bake in a greased 11 x 15" pan at 350° for 20 min.

FROSTING:
- 3 oz. cream cheese
- 6 Tbsp. butter
- 1 Tbsp. milk
- 3 1/2 c. powdered sugar
- 1 tsp. vanilla

SOUR CREAM RAISIN BARS

- 2 3/4 c. quick oatmeal
- 1 1/2 c. brown sugar
- 1 c. and 5 Tbsp. oleo
- 1 1/4 c. white sugar
- 2 c. sour cream
- 2 3/4 c. pastry flour
- 1 1/2 tsp. baking powder
- 4 egg yolks
- 1 Tbsp. cornstarch
- 2 c. raisins

Mix together oatmeal, flour, brown sugar, baking powder and oleo. Bake 2/3 of crumbs in a cake pan at 350° for 2 min. Cool. Mix egg yolks, white sugar, cornstarch, sour cream, and raisins. Pour over top of crust and add remaining crumbs. Bake until done, about 30 min.

RAISIN TOP COOKIES

2 c. brown sugar
1 c. shortening
2 eggs
4 c. flour
1 tsp. soda
1 tsp. salt
4 Tbsp. milk
1 Tbsp. vanilla

Have dough stiff enough to roll in little balls the size of a walnut. Place on baking sheet and make a little dish with your finger to put in filling.

FILLING:

3/4 c. raisins
1/2 c. white sugar
1 1/2 c. water
salt

Cook one half hour then thicken with 1 Tbsp. clear jel. Add maple flavoring to suit your taste. Cherries or pineapple can also be used.

Mrs. Mary Ellen Wengerd

RAISIN BARS

1 c. raisins
1 c. water
1 1/2 tsp. soda
1/2 tsp. salt
1/2 c. oleo
1 egg
1 c. sugar
2 c. flour
1 tsp. cinnamon
1/2 c. nuts
vanilla

Cook raisins and water until tender. Cool and add 1/2 teaspoon soda, salt, and oleo. Cream egg with sugar. Sift together flour, 1 tsp. soda, and cinnamon. Mix flour mixture to raisins, then add egg and sugar combination. Fold in nuts and vanilla. Spread on a greased and floured jelly roll pan. Bake at 350° for 20 min.

GLAZE:

1/2 stick oleo

Add powdered sugar and water until spreading consistency.

Ruby Beachy

MOLASSES COOKIES

1 c. brown sugar
1 c. shortening
1 c. molasses
1 tsp. salt
2 eggs, beaten
1 c. buttermilk
4 c. flour
4 tsp. soda
2 tsp. cinnamon
1/2 tsp. cloves or
1/2 tsp. nutmeg
1 c. nuts, optional

Mix in order given. Drop by tsp. on baking sheet. Bake at 350° for about 10 min.

Mrs. (Junior) Edna Miller

SOFT MOLASSES COOKIES

3/4 c. vegetable oil	3/4 c. brown sugar
3/4 c. molasses	2 eggs, beaten
3/4 c. sour cream	2 1/2 c. flour
1/2 tsp. salt	2 tsp. baking soda
1/2 tsp. cinnamon	1 1/2 tsp. ginger

Cream oil and sugar. Add well beaten eggs, molasses, and sour cream. Stir until smooth. Add dry ingredients gradually to mixture. Chill dough, then drop by spoonfuls on baking sheets. Bake at 350° until light brown.

SOFT GINGER DROPS

1/2 c. shortening	1 tsp. cinnamon
3/4 c. sugar	2 tsp. ginger
1 egg	1 tsp. nutmeg
1 1/4 c. molasses	1 tsp. cloves
4 1/2 c. flour	1 c. boiling water
2 tsp. soda	

Combine shortening, sugar, egg, and molasses. Sift together dry ingredients and add to mixture, then add water. Drop on baking sheet. Bake at 400°.

FROSTING:

2 c. powdered sugar	1 tsp. lemon extract
1 Tbsp. butter, softened	3 Tbsp. milk

Mrs. Margaret Yoder

HONEY COOKIES

1 c. oleo	1/2 tsp. cinnamon
2 c. honey	1/2 tsp. all spice
4 tsp. soda	2 tsp. vanilla
2 eggs, beaten	6 1/2 or more c. flour

Boil oleo and honey for 1 min. Remove from heat and add soda. Cool and put in large bowl, then add eggs, cinnamon, all spice, vanilla, and flour. Roll out thin like cut-outs and cut with your favorite cookie cutter. Bake at 350°.

ICING:

5 tsp. boiling water	2 egg whites, beaten
1 1/3 c. sugar	

Beat until stiff. Spread over cooled cookies. Can also use crisco frosting.

ORANGE COOKIES

1 c. sugar
1 c. shortening
2 eggs
1/2 tsp. salt
4 c. flour
1 c. sour cream
1 tsp. soda
1 tsp. vanilla

No need to refrigerate before rolling out dough.

Mrs. Sevilla Miller

ORANGE COOKIES

2 c. white sugar
1 c. shortening, butter, or lard
1 c. sour milk or buttermilk
juice of 1 orange
1 grated orange rind
1 tsp. soda
2 tsp. baking powder
4 c. flour (more or less)

Cream together sugar, shortening, milk, juice of orange and orange rind. Mix together soda, baking powder and flour. Add to creamed mixture and blend well. Drop with spoon on cookie sheet. Bake at 350° until done. Ice with your favorite icing.

Nora Yoder

OUTRAGEOUS CHOCOLATE CHIP COOKIES

1 c. oleo
1 c. white sugar
2/3 c. brown sugar
1 c. peanut butter
1 tsp. vanilla
2 eggs
2 c. Robin Hood flour
1 c. quick oats
2 tsp. soda
1/2 tsp. salt
1 c. chocolate chips

Preheat oven to 350°. Beat oleo, sugars, peanut butter, vanilla, and eggs in a large bowl until creamy and well blended. Mix in flour, oats, soda, and salt. Stir in chocolate chips. Drop by rounded teaspoonful on floured cookie sheet. Bake 10 to 12 min. or until golden brown. Cool 1 min. before removing from cookie sheet. If you don't put oats in, add 2/3 c. flour. Very good! Yield: 4 dozen.

Alma Hershberger, Mrs. Anna Troyer

~ *To lengthen thy life, lessen thy meals.* ~

DOUBLE CHOCOLATE CHIP COOKIES

3 c. sugar	2 1/2 c. flour
1 c. oleo	2 tsp. soda
1 c. lard	2 tsp. salt
2 eggs	2 tsp. vanilla
1/2 c. water	5 c. oatmeal
2/3 c. cocoa	12 oz. chocolate chips

ICING:
Beat together:

2 egg whites	4 tsp. vanilla
4 tsp. milk	2 c. powdered sugar
4 tsp. flour	

Add 2 more c. powdered sugar and 1 1/2 c. crisco. Blend until smooth. Spread between 2 cookies.

Mrs. Sevilla Miller

CHOCOLATE CHIP COOKIES

2 1/4 c. flour	1 pkg. vanilla instant pudding
1 tsp. baking soda	1 tsp. vanilla
1 c. butter or oleo	2 eggs, beaten
3/4 c. brown sugar	12 oz. chocolate chips

Mix together all ingredients, adding chips last. Drop on cookie sheet and bake at 350° for 10 min.

Mrs. Miriam Miller

CLASSIC CHOCOLATE CHIP COOKIES

2 1/2 c. all-purpose flour	1 pkg. instant vanilla pudding
1 tsp. baking soda	2 eggs
1 c. margarine, softened	12 oz. semi sweet chocolate chips
1/4 c. sugar	1 c. chopped nuts, optional
3/4 c. brown sugar, firmly packed	

Combine flour and baking soda. Set aside. Mix together butter, sugars, vanilla, and pudding mix in a large bowl. Beat until smooth and creamy. Beat in eggs. Gradually add flour mixture. Stir in chocolate chips and nuts. Batter will be stiff. Bake at 375° for 9 to 10 min. or until browned. Yield: 4 1/2 dozen.

Marie Kline

CHOCOLATE CHIP COOKIES

2 c. white sugar	2 pkg. vanilla instant
2 c. margarine	pudding
4 eggs	2 tsp. soda
2 tsp. vanilla	4 1/2 c. flour
1 tsp. salt	2 c. chocolate chips

Beat together sugar and margarine until creamy. Add eggs and beat well. Add vanilla, salt, dry pudding mix, and soda. Stir in flour. Lastly, stir in chocolate chips. Drop by spoonsful onto lightly floured cookie sheet. Bake at 350°. Do not overbake.

Marie Troyer

CHEWY BROWNIE COOKIES

2/3 c. crisco shortening	1 1/2 c. all-purpose flour
1 1/2 c. brown sugar	1/3 c. Hershey's cocoa
1 Tbsp. water	1/4 tsp. baking soda
1 tsp. vanilla	1/2 tsp. salt
2 eggs	2 c. chocolate chips

Heat oven to 375°. Combine crisco, sugar, water, and vanilla in large bowl. Beat until well blended. Beat eggs into creamed mixture. Combine flour, cocoa, salt, and baking soda. Mix into creamed mixture. Stir in chocolate chips. Bake for 7 to 9 min. Do not overbake. Cool 2 min. on baking sheet. Yield: About 3 dozen.

CHOCOLATE CHIP COOKIES

2 1/2 c. flour	1 tsp. vanilla
1 tsp. soda	1 pkg. vanilla instant
1 c. margarine	pudding
1/4 c. white sugar	2 eggs
3/4 c. brown sugar	4 oz. chocolate chips

Cream together margarine and sugar, add soda, eggs, vanilla, and flour. Add rest of ingredients. Drop by teaspoons on greased cookie sheets. Bake at 350° for 5 min.

Diane Keim

~ Knowledge comes, but wisdom lingers. ~

CHOCOLATE CHIP BARS

1 1/2 c. brown sugar
2 eggs
1 1/2 tsp. baking powder
1/2 c. chopped nuts
2/3 c. oil
1 tsp. vanilla
1 tsp. salt
1 1/2 c. flour

Beat eggs until thick and foamy. Add sugar. Beat well, add oil and vanilla. Blend in flour, baking powder, salt and chocolate chips. Bake at 350° for 25 min.

THUMB PRINT COOKIES

1/4 c. shortening
1/4 c. butter, softened
1/4 c. brown sugar
3/4 c. chopped nuts
1 egg yolk
1/2 tsp. vanilla
1/4 tsp. salt
1 c. flour

Mix together shortening, butter, brown sugar, egg yolk, & vanilla. Add salt & flour. Roll dough into balls. Beat egg whites slightly & roll ball of dough into egg whites & then roll into chopped nuts. Bake for 5 min. at 375°. Remove from oven & press thumb into center of cookie. Return to oven for about 3 min. or until done baking. Frost centers of cookies.

MEXICAN WEDDING CAKES

1 c. soft butter
1/2 c. powdered sugar
1 1/2 tsp. vanilla
2 1/4 c. sifted flour
1 c. chopped nuts

Cream butter & sugar. Add flour & vanilla. Mix in nuts. Chill batter. Roll in 1/2" balls. Bake at 350° for 12 to 15 min. Roll in powdered sugar while still warm.

PECAN PUFFS

1 c. crisco
1/2 c. powdered sugar
2 1/4 c. flour
1 tsp. vanilla
1/2 tsp. salt
1/4 c. chopped pecans

Cream crisco & powdered sugar. Stir in flour, salt, vanilla, & pecans. Blend well. Roll into 1" balls. Place on greased cookie sheet. Bake at 375°. Roll in powdered sugar. The dough can also be rolled out like for cut-outs & cut with a star or half moon cookie cutter.

Nora Yoder

CHRISTMAS CUT-OUTS COOKIES

2 c. oleo
3 c. white sugar
5 eggs, beaten
1 c. sour cream
1 tsp. soda
1 tsp. vanilla
1 tsp. baking powder
1/4 c. boiling water
6 1/2 c. flour

Blend oleo and sugar. Add beaten eggs and sour cream. Stir in boiling water. Mix well and add dry ingredients. Chill dough. Roll and cut out. Bake at 350° to 375°.

VALENTINE BUTTER COOKIES

2 c. butter, softened
2 c. sugar
3 eggs
1 Tbsp. vanilla extract
6 c. all-purpose flour
2 tsp. baking powder
red decorator's sugar, optional

In a mixing bowl, cream butter and sugar. Add eggs and vanilla; mix well. Combine flour and baking powder. Gradually add to creamed mixture and mix well. Shape with a cookie press. Place on ungreased cookie sheets. Decorate with sugar if desired. Bake at 350° for 10 to 12 min. or until edges are light brown. Yield: 18 - 19 doz.

~ If you can't make it better, you can laugh at it. ~

My Favorite Recipes:

My Favorite Recipes:

Snacks and Misc.

SOFT PRETZELS

1 Tbsp. dry yeast
1 1/3 c. warm water
4 tsp. sugar
1/2 tsp. salt
4 c. unsifted flour
1 1/2 Tbsp. butter
coarse salt

Preheat oven to 400°. Dissolve yeast in warm water. Add sugar and salt. Gradually blend in 3 c. flour. Knead in remaining flour until smooth. Tear dough into 12 equal pieces. Roll each piece into a rope about 15" long. Shape into a pretzel. Melt butter and brush on pretzels. Sprinkle with coarse salt. Bake 12 to 15 min. or until golden brown on an ungreased cookie sheet. Six pretzels per cookie sheet.

Mrs. Margaret Yoder

VEGETABLE PIZZA

2 pkgs. crescent rolls
1/2 c. miracle whip
2 (8 oz.) pkgs. cream cheese
1 pkg. ranch dressing mix

Separate crescent rolls. Press in a pan. Bake as directed. Mix cream cheese, miracle whip and ranch mix together. Spread over cooled crust. Sprinkle with bacon, broccoli, cheese, carrots or vegetables of your choice.

Karen Raber

VEGETABLE BARS

2 (8 oz.) pkgs. crescent rolls
2 (8 oz.) pkgs. cream cheese
1 pkg. Hidden Valley ranch dressing mix
2 (8 oz.) sour cream

Spread rolls on large cookie sheet. Bake at 350° for 7 to 8 min. Cool for 10 min. Mix together rest of ingredients and spread over rolls. Top with broccoli, cauliflower, carrots, and grated cheese. Press vegetables firmly into cream cheese mixture.

Nancy Miller

~ Little drops of water, little grains of sand, make the mighty ocean and the pleasant land. ~

FINGER JELLO

4 pkgs. jello
4 Tbsp. gelatin
1/2 c. cold water
3 c. boiling water
2 c. cold water
a little sugar

Soak gelatin in 1/2 c. cold water. Add to jello mixture. Pour in a pan and let cool.

Linda Miller

FINGER JELLO

6 oz. jello
2 c. boiling water
White Part:
1 can eagle brand milk
2 c. boiling water
1 pkg. Knox gelatin

4 pkgs. Knox gelatin

Put in layers of red, white and green. Let one layer set before you put another layer on.

Mrs. Sue Miller

PINWHEEL FINGER JELLO

3 oz. jello, any flavor
3/4 c. hot water
2 c. mini marshmallows

Spray an 8" square pan with cooking spray. Spread over sides and bottom with a paper towel. Mix jello and hot water until jello is dissolved. Add marshmallows and stir until marshmallows are mostly dissolved. Pour into pan and refrigerate till set. Loosen edges with a knife and roll up like a jelly roll. Cut in slices.

Mrs. (Henry) Edna Miller

FINGER JELLO

4 env. Knox gelatin
3 pkgs. jello
5 c. boiling water
1 1/2 c. cold water

Combine gelatins. Add boiling water and stir until dissolved. Add cold water. Chill until firm. Use a 9 x 13" pan. Yield: about 100 1" cubes.

Mrs. Miriam Miller

CINNAMON POPCORN

13 qt. bowl freshly popped corn
1 c. white sugar
1 c. cinnamon imperials
1/2 c. white karo
1 tsp. salt
1 c. margarine
1 tsp. vanilla
1/2 tsp. baking soda

In a heavy saucepan, boil margarine, sugar, karo, cinnamon imperials, and salt for 5 min. Add vanilla and baking soda. Stir well. Pour over popcorn and mix well. Place on cookie sheets and bake one hour at 250°, stirring every 10 to 15 min.

CARAMEL CORN

1 gal. popped corn
1 c. brown sugar
1 stick oleo
1/4 c. white karo
1/4 tsp. soda
1/2 tsp. vanilla

Cook sugar, oleo, and karo for 4 min. Remove from heat. Add soda and vanilla. Pour over popcorn and stir until evenly coated. Bake on a greased cookie sheet or large pan at 225° for 1 hour. Break apart.

Mrs. (Henry) Edna Miller

CRISPY CARAMEL CORN

3 1/2 qts. popped corn
1/2 c. butter or margarine
1 c. light brown sugar
1/4 c. light corn syrup
1/2 tsp. salt
1/2 tsp. vanilla
1/4 tsp. soda

Place popped corn in a large, well-greased pan. In a saucepan melt butter. Stir in sugar, syrup and salt and boil for 5 min. over med. heat. Remove from heat and stir in soda and vanilla. Pour over popcorn, mixing well. Bake at 350° for 1 hour, stirring every 15 min. When cool, separate kernels. Store in a tightly covered container.

Mrs. Miriam Miller

~ Work is the yeast that raises the dough. ~

PEANUT BRITTLE

3/4 c. white sugar
3/4 c. brown sugar
1/2 c. light karo
1/4 c. water

2 c. peanuts
1 1/2 tsp. soda
1/4 tsp. salt

In a saucepan combine sugar, karo, and water. Bring to a boil. Stir in peanuts and keep a rolling boil until peanuts pop and turn brown. Remove from heat. Add soda and stir well. Add salt. Pour in a greased pan. Cool. Break in pieces.

Susie Yoder

SMORE'S

Graham crackers
Large marshmallows

Peanut butter
Hershey's milk chocolate candy bars

Break each graham cracker into 4 pieces. Cut each marshmallow in half and roast over a fire until soft. Put 2 halves on graham cracker that has been spread with peanut butter. Place a piece of the candy bar on marshmallows and spread peanut butter on candy bar. Top with another cracker.

COCONUT BIRD NESTS

12 oz. chocolate pieces
14 oz. pkg. sweetened coconut

12 oz. pkg. almond
M & M's

Melt chocolate in double boiler. Add coconut. Drop heaping tablespoons on wax paper to form nest; press with back of spoon to hollow out and shape each nest. Press 4 to 5 M & M's in the center of each nest. Place in a cool place until firm.

PEANUT BUTTER CANDY COOKIES

1/2 c. brown sugar
1/2 c. peanut butter

1/4 c. evaporated milk
2 1/2 c. rice crispy cereal

In a medium saucepan combine brown sugar, peanut butter and milk. Bring to boiling, stirring constantly until sugar is dissolved, and peanut butter is melted. Remove from heat and stir in cereal. Drop on waxed paper. Yield: about 3 doz.

CHICKEN IN A BISCUIT CRACKERS

12 c. oyster crackers
2 Tbsp. dry chicken base
2 Tbsp. sour cream & onion powder
1 c. wesson oil

Mix together real well. Bake for 1/2 hour at 300°. Stir every couple min.

Mrs. Lizzie Keim

PUPPY CHOW

1 c. chocolate chips
3/4 c. peanut butter
1/4 c. butter

Mix above ingredients together and microwave until smooth. Do not let it get too hot. Pour mixture over 8 c. Crispex cereal. Toss until cereal is coated. Sprinkle 2 c. powdered sugar over coated cereal.

Mary Anna Troyer

PARTY MIX

1 box Rice Chex
1 box Corn Chex or Wheat Chex
1 box Kix
1 box Honey Combs
M & M's
2 lbs. nuts
2 bags pretzel sticks

Sauce:
2 c. Wesson oil
2 Tbsp. Lawry's salt
4 Tbsp. worcestershire sauce

Place in 2 roasters, all except M & M's. Bake at 250° for 2 - 3 hours stirring every 15 min., adding more sauce each time. Pour in M & M's when cool.

RICE KRISPIE TREATS

1/4 c. butter
4 c. miniature marshmallows
5 c. Rice Krispies Cereal

Melt margarine. Add marshmallows and stir until all are melted. Pour over rice krispies and stir until evenly coated. Spread in a greased 9 x 13" pan.

~ *You can be young only once but can be immature forever.* ~

COOL WHIP TREAT

2 1/4 c. chocolate ice cream wafer cookie crumbs, divided
1/2 c. sugar, divided
1/2 c. margarine, melted
8 oz. cream cheese, softened
12 oz. cool whip
2 c. boiling water
2 pkgs. (4 serving size) orange jello
1/2 c. cold water
ice cubes

Mix 2 c. of the cookie crumbs, 1/4 c. of the sugar and margarine together. Press into a 9 x 13 pan. Refrigerate. Beat cream cheese and remaining sugar in a bowl until smooth. Stir in 1/2 of the whipped topping. Spread over crust. Stir boiling water into gelatin until dissolved. Mix cold water and ice to make 1 1/2 c. Stir into gelatin until slightly thickened. Remove any remaining ice. Spoon over cream cheese layer. Refrigerate until firm. Spread remaining whipped topping over gelatin mixture. Sprinkle with remaining cookie crumbs.

REESE'S TEMPTATIONS

1/2 c. margarine
1/2 c. peanut butter
1/2 c. sugar
1/2 c. brown sugar
1 egg
1 tsp. vanilla
1/2 tsp. salt
1 1/2 c. flour
3/4 tsp. baking soda

Form into 1" balls and place in ungreased miniature muffin pan. Bake at 375° for 8 to 10 min. Remove from oven and place 1 miniature Reese's Cup in center of each. Let cool for 10 min. and remove from pan. Yield: 4 to 5 doz.

FANTASY FUDGE

6 c. sugar
1 1/2 c. margarine
1 1/3 c. evaporated milk
2 (12 oz.) pkgs. choclate chips
13 oz. jar Kraft marshmallow creme
2 c. chopped nuts
2 tsp. vanilla

Stir together sugar, margarine and milk in a heavy 5 qt. saucepan. Bring to a full boil, stirring constantly. Boil for 5 min. over medium heat or until candy thermometer reaches 234°. Stir constantly to prevent scorching. Remove from heat. Gradually stir in chocolate chips until melted. Add remaining ingredients. Mix until well blended. Pour into 2 greased 9 x 9" or 9 x 13" pans. Cool at room temperature and cut into squares. Yield: 6 pounds.

Mrs. Miriam Miller

FUDGE BARS
4 c. miniature marshmallows   3 qts. popped popcorn
1 c. butterscotch chips   12 oz. jar hot fudge sauce
3 Tbsp. butter

In a large Dutch oven, over low heat, melt marshmallows with butterscotch chips and butter. Stir occasionally until smooth. Add popcorn. Toss until well coated. Press half of mixture firmly into a greased 9" square pan. Spread fudge sauce evenly over mixture. Press remaining popcorn mixture over fudge. Allow mixture to cool and harden. Slide spatula under entire mixture and slide onto cutting board to cut into squares. Yield: 16 bars.

STRAWBERRY JAM
4 c. strawberries, mashed   4 c. sugar

Cook for 13 min. Add a dot of butter to eliminate the foam that forms. Pour into jars, screw on lids, turn upside down to seal.

QUICK STRAWBERRY JAM
3 c. mashed strawberries   3 c. sugar

Combine and let stand for four hours. Then in a heavy saucepan heat to boiling. Reduce heat and boil for 10 min.

3 oz. pkg. gelatin

Stir gelatin into strawberry mixture until dissolved. Bring to a boiling point. Remove from heat and let set a few min. Stir mixture again; ladle into clean jelly or 1/2 pint jars or containers. Store in refrigerator or freezer. Yield: 6 to 8 1/2 pints.

PEACHY ORANGE JAM
Grate rinds of:
3 large juicy oranges   1 lemon

Squeeze the juice from the fruit and remove the seeds; do not strain. Combine rinds and juices in a large heavy saucepan.

Add to pan:
3 lbs. peaches, peeled and chopped

Stir in:
6 c. sugar

Bring mixture to a boil over medium heat, stirring often. Reduce heat and let simmer, uncovered, until thickened, about 35 to 40 min., stir frequently. Pour jam into hot, sterilized jars and seal. Process in a boiling water bath for 5 min. after water returns to boiling.

AMISH CHURCH PEANUT BUTTER

8 c. brown sugar
3 3/4 c. water
2 1/2 tsp. maple flavoring
3/4 c. karo

Boil, remove from heat. Cool to lukewarm. Mix in 5 to 6 pounds peanut butter and 2 to 3 quarts marshmallow topping.

Barbara Troyer

PEANUT BUTTER SANDWICH SPREAD

2 c. brown sugar
1 c. water
2 Tbsp. karo
1 tsp. maple flavoring

Bring to a boil. Cool. Add 1 jar marshmallow creme and 2 c. peanut butter. Mix.

Ruby Beachy

APPLE BUTTER

3 qts. unsweetened applesauce
2 c. white sugar
2 c. brown sugar
1 tsp. cinnamon
1/2 tsp. ground cloves
1/4 tsp. allspice

Mix ingredients all together and bake until thick at 325° to 350°. Remove from oven and add 3 tsp. vinegar if desired. Put in jars and water bath for 20 min.

Mrs. Ida Miller

GOOD PICKLES

1 gallon sliced pickles

Soak in cold water and 1 c. salt for 4 days. On the fourth day rinse off and put into kettle. Cover with cold water and add 1 heaping tablespoon alum and boil ten min. Rinse off and cover with cold water. Add teaspoon ginger and boil ten min. Rinse and put in the following syrup.

SYRUP:

6 c. sugar
1 pint water
1 pint vinegar
1 tsp. salt

Put 1 Tbsp. pickling spice in a cloth bag and boil for 30 min.

Mrs. Ora Lena Miller

~ Patience is a necessary ingredient for success. ~

SWEET DILL PICKLES

Pickles
3 c. sugar
3 c. water
1 c. vinegar
2 tsp. salt
1 1/2 tsp. dill weed

Slice the pickles and put in jars. Heat the rest of ingredients and pour over pickles. Cold pack until just boiling. Take out of canner.

Mrs. Ida Miller

JOGGIN' IN A JUG

1 qt. apple juice, unsweetened
1 qt. grape juice, unsweetened
1 c. vinegar (Heinz)

Drink 2 oz. a day to help keep your cholesterol in check.

Mrs. Ida Miller

CHOCOLATE MARSHMALLOW SAUCE

1/2 c. milk
1/4 c. butter
1/8 tsp. salt
1 c. semi-sweet chocolate morsels
1 tsp. vanilla
1 pint jar marshmallow creme

Combine milk, butter, and salt. Bring just to a boil over medium heat, stirring constantly. Remove from heat and stir in morsels and vanilla. Stir until smooth and blended. Blend in marshmallow creme. Serve over cake or ice cream.

FISH BATTER

1 egg white
3 tsp. baking powder
1 tsp. oil
1 tsp. salt
1 c. flour
3 1/2 lbs. fish

Beat egg white until stiff. Mix remaining ingredients with 3/4 c. water then add to egg white. Dip fish into mixture and fry.

YOGURT

2 qts. milk
2 Tbsp. yogurt
1 Tbsp. vanilla
1 pkg. plain gelatin
1 c. sugar

Heat milk to 190°. Dissolve gelatin in small amount of cold water. When milk is cooled to 130° add other ingredients and stir well with wire whip. Keep a 110° for 8 hours or overnite.

Mary Anna Troyer

WHITE SAUCE

2 Tbsp. butter
1/4 tsp. salt
2 Tbsp. flour
1 1/2 - 2 c. milk

Melt butter. Add salt. Stir in flour. Slowly stir in milk. Stir and cook until thickened.

CORN SALAD

40 ears corn, cooked and cut off kernels
1/2 c. salt
2 bunches celery
2 medium cabbage heads
2 Tbsp. cornstarch
1 1/2 qt. vinegar, may be part water to suit taste
1 pint water
8 medium onions
4 sweet peppers, any or all colors
3 to 4 c. sugar
1 Tbsp. dry mustard
1 Tbsp. tumeric

Shred or cut all vegetables in small pieces. Mix all ingredients well. Boil 10 min., stirring constantly. Pack in jars. Seal and cold pack about 1 hour in water bath or 15 min. at 10 lbs. pressure in pressure cooker.

Alma Hershberger

BEST BIG BATCH TOMATO SAUCE (TO CAN)

1/4 c. salad oil
3 onions, sliced
3 carrots, diced
2 garlic cloves, minced
12 tomatoes, peeled & diced
2 green peppers, diced
12 oz. can tomato paste
1/4 c. brown sugar
2 Tbsp. salt
2 tsp. oregano flakes
1 1/2 tsp. basil flakes
1/2 tsp. pepper

Over medium heat, in hot salad oil cook onions, carrots, peppers, and garlic until tender, stirring occasionally. Add remaining ingredients. Cook over high heat to boiling. Reduce heat to med., cover partially and cook for 2 hours. Cold pack for 45 min. Thicken with clear jel if desired. Yield: 9 pints.

Sarah Yoder

~ *Success is a journey, not a destination.* ~

My Favorite Recipes:

My Favorite Recipes:

Amish Lifestyle

Jakie Miller groaned
   as he heard Mom call once more;
No more snoozing, now she means it,
   time to go help chore.
Since they had no electric
   he just dressed in the dark,
For Jakie is an Amish boy,
   from the world they're set apart.
After helping milk the cows
   he ate breakfast with the family.
Their house is furnished simply,
   no extra frills or fancies.

He walked to school just down the road
   a little o're a mile.
Teacher Mary greeted him
   with her usual sunny smile.
She had a fire going,
   her lessons all prepared.
To teach eight grades takes patience
   and skill beyond compare.
There's just one room no indoor plumbing,
   the basic needs, that's all.
School only lasts til April
   there's work at home til fall.

The bell has rung and teacher
   begins with first grade reading.
Yesterday Jake stayed at home
   and now he starts a dreaming:
It was such fun to have the thrashers
   at their place for the day.
Ten men were in the ring
   in which his father helped thrash grain.
As they worked a few of them
   played tricks upon each other.

Jakie was all eyes and ears,
    these men were just like brothers.
Mom fixed a large but simple lunch,
    they sure put food away,
Then back to work to finish up
    before the end of day.
"Jakie, is your grammar done?
    If you daydream one more time
You'll stay in at recess,
    You must learn to mind!"

The day is finally over,
    As Jake walks up their yard
He sees a van and buggies
    parked out by the barn.
Mom has a cousin quilting,
    he shyly goes inside.
They're all so busy visiting
    as the needles fly.
The quilt is for big sister,
    Jake thinks she'll soon be wed,
The way they're fixed up everything,
    even built a shed.

On Saturday quite early
    they went to neighbor Dans.
Their barn burned down last week
    So a barnraising was planned.
They're expecting lots of people,
    from four to seven hundred.
Some women come to help to cook
    but the men have them outnumbered.
By evening they're all finished,
    that new barn sure looks grand!
Just goes to show what can be done
    by willing hearts and hands.

On Sunday they all dress up
    in their Sunday best.
Then off to church, this is the day
    of worship and of rest.
They go with horse and buggy,
    they're on their way by eight.
They hope to get there early,
    to be tardy's a disgrace.
For church, they all take turns,
    in their homes they get together.
Either in the house or barn,
    depends upon the weather.
It is a three-hour service,
    on benches with no backs.
Half way through small children
    have a pretzel-cookie snack.
They announced the engagement
    of big sister and her friend.
In two weeks they'll be married,
    on that you can depend.
After church is over
    they serve a simple lunch
Of bread and spreads and coldcuts
    and cookies for to munch.
They stay and visit for awhile
    no hurry to go home;
For here they hear the latest news,
    they have no cars or phones.

After the engagement
    at church has been announced
The wedding ceremony
    is held at the bride's house.
The cooks, I'm told, are Mom's choice,
    she usually chooses ten.
They come and help the week before
    prepare for this event.
There's chicken, mashed potatoes, salads
    cakes and pies.
The servers are all relatives
    or good friends of the bride.

I hope this brief account
   will help you understand
The lifestyle of the Amish
   in some ways it is grand.
            - Written by - Cousin Ruth Miller

Appetizers, Beverages, and Dips 7
Best Ever Punch 9
Cheese Ball 8
Cheese Dip 10
Citrus Dip 11
Crunchy Swiss & Ham Appetizers ... 8
Fresh Fruit Dip 11
Fruit Dip 11
Fruit Slush 8
Golden Punch 9
Hamburger Cheese Dip 10
Hot Chocolate Mix 10
Orange Sherbet Punch 9
Party Punch 9
Salsa 12
Slush Drink 9
Taffy Apple Dip 11
Vegetable Dip 12
Warm Taco Dip 10

Breakfast 15
Baked Oatmeal 23
Best Ever Biscuits 20
Baked Stuffed Eggs 24
Blueberry Oat Muffins 19
Bran Biscuits 20
Breakfast Casserole 17
Breakfast Pizza 17
Buttermilk Biscuits 21
Cheese Muffins 20
Corn Meal Mush 23
Deluxe Honey Nut Granola 23
Feather - Light Muffins 18
French Toast 22
Fried Cornmeal Mush 24
Grandma's Apple Muffins 19
Grapenuts 22
Ham and Cheese Omelet 16
Light Pancakes 22
Oatmeal Apple Raisin Muffins 18
Onion Cake 16
Orange Corn Muffins 18
Pancakes 21, 22
Potato Pancakes 22
Sausage Gravy 23

Sheep Herder's Breakfast 16
Tacoed Eggs 24

Bread, Rolls, and Pastries . 27
Brown Bread 29
Buns 31
Butter Tarts 35
Cream Sticks 34
Delicious Apple Bread 33
Dinner Rolls 30
Doughnuts 35
Easy French Bread 32
Filled Butter Horns 36
Golden Cornbread 31
Homemade Bread 28
2 Hour Dinner Rolls 30
Mexican Cornbread 32
Mom's Bread 28
Monkey Bread 29
Overnight Cinnamon Rolls 34
Quick Dinner Buns 30
Simple Doughnuts 35
Spoon Bread 31
Sweet Rolls 31
Toasty Garlic Bread 32
White Bread 28
Whole Wheat Bread 29
Zucchini Bread 33

Main Dishes & Vegetables . 39
Baked Bean Casserole 70
Baked Creamed Corn 71
Ballard Biscuits 57
Bar-B-Q Hamburgers 46
Bar-B-Q Meat Balls 45
BBQ Sauce 40
BBQ Sauce for Ham 40
Bar-B-Q Steak 43
Beef and Cheese Enchiladas 59
Beef and Macaroni 54
Cabbage Casserole 71
Cajun Cabbage 71
Calico Beans 70
California Rice 69
Cheeseburger Pie 55
Cheese Hashbrowns 65

214

Cheesy Rice Patties	69
Chicken and Biscuit Casserole	50
Chicken and Rice	54
Chicken Barbecue Sauce	40
Chicken Enchilada	57
Chicken Fried Steak	43
Chicken Gumbo	51
Coney Sauce	40
Crescent Cheeseburger Pie	56
Crescent Roll Lasagna	60
Crockpot Supper	55
Company Casserole	49
Dandelion	72
Delicious BBQ Chicken	41
Dried Beef Casserole	52
Easy Mashed Potatoes	68
Easy Scalloped Potatoes	66
Ella's Awesome Chicken	41
El-Paso Casserole	48
German Pizza	64
Ground Beef Grandstyle	47
Grilled Potatoes	68
Gypsy Spaghetti	61
Ham Loaf	43, 44
Haystack	58
Honey Mustard Chicken	42
Hungarian Chicken	42
Irish Italian Spaghetti	61
Jiffy Pizza Dough	63
Jr.'s Favorite	54
Lasagna	60
Macaroni and Chicken Casserole	52
Macaroni with Beef and Beans	55
Meat Balls in Gravy	45
Meat Loaf	44, 45
Mexican Casserole	48
$25,00 Mexican Dish	59
Mexican Goulash	48
Mock Ham Loaf	43
One Skillet Spaghetti	62
Oven Barbecued Chicken	41
Pansy Supper Casserole	47
Paprika Potatoes	65
Pizza Burgers	63
Pizza Crust	63
Pizza Casserole	53
Pizza Cups	62
Pizza Dough	63
Poor Man's Steak	42, 43
Pork Chop Spaghetti	61
Pork Chops with Scalloped Potatoes	58
Potluck Potatoes	66, 67
Potato Puffs	68
Quick Cheeseburger Bake	56
Rice Casserole	69
Rigatoni	50
Salmon Loaf	57
Sarah's Chicken Dressing	54
Sauce for Meatloaf, Chicken, and Hamburgers	40
Sausage Casserole	52
Savory Meatballs	46
Scalloped Corn	70
Scalloped Potatoes	66
Ship Wreck	47
Sizzle Burgers	46
Sloppy Joes	64, 65
Sour Cream Noodle Casserole	49
Sour Kraut (to can)	71
Spaghetti Supreme	62
Spinach Mashed Potatoes	67
Stromboli	59
Sweet Potatoes	65
Taco Casserole	50
Taco Pie	57
Tator Tot Casserole	52
Tostados	58
Turkey Casserole	51
Underground Ham Casserole	51
Upside Down Pizza	64
Western Beans	70
Yum-A-Setta	47

Soups, Salads, and Dressings ... 75

Broccoli Salad	88
Buttery Onion Soup	79
Cheesy Chicken Chowder	80
Cheesy Vegetable Soup	77
Chicken Noodle Soup	76
Chili Soup	79
Cottage Cheese Salad	85
Cranberry Salad	85

Cream Cheese Salad 82	Cream Cheese Pie 111
Cream of Broccoli Soup 78	Creamy Cool Cheesecake 111
Creamy Tomato Soup 79	Cream Filled Chocolate Cookie
Easy Broccoli Soup 78	Ice Cream Pie 96
Easy Potato Soup 76	Cream Puffs 112
Fish and Cheese Chowder 80	Date Pudding 105
French Dressing 89	Delicious Custard 108
Frozen Waldorf Salad 85	Dirt Pudding 104
Green Salad 85	Florida Pudding 95
Hearty Hamburger Soup 77	Fluff Pudding 101
Hearty Ham Soup 78	Fried Ice Cream 114
Indiana Salad 81	Frozen Cheese Cake 111
Kool Whip Salad 83	Fruit Dessert 98
Laura's Dressing 90	Fruit Pizza 98
Lime Salad 81	Golden Brown Apple
Macaroni Salad 86	Dumplings 107
Orange Danish 81	Goody Pudding 101
Orange Salad 84	Hawaiian Pineapple Pudding 100
Potato Salad 86, 87	Heath Bar Dessert 102
Quick Fruit Salad 81	Homemade Ice Cream 115
Quick Vegetable Soup 77	Hot Fudge Pudding 96
Rainbow Salad 84	Ice Cream 115
Ribbon Salad 82	Ice Cream Pudding 102
Seven Layer Salad 89	Jello Pudding 97
Sour Cream Dressing 90	Jelly Roll 114
Sweet and Sour Dressing 89	Lemon Apple Dumplings 106
Taco Salad 87, 88	Lemon Cream Cheese Pie 110
Tapioca 82, 83	Lemon Delight 94
Thousand Island Dressing 89	Old Fashioned Cracker
Tortilla Soup 80	Pudding 102
Triple Orange Salad 84	Oreo Cookie Pudding 103
7 - Up Salad 83	Oreo Mint Pudding 104
Warm Taco Salad 87	Oreo Pudding 104
	Our Favorite Ice Cream 114
Desserts 93	Peaches and Cream Cheese
Abby's Rice Pudding 107	Cake 110
Angel Food Cake Dessert . 107, 108	Pistachio Pudding 103
Angel Food Dessert 108	Pretzel Dessert 99
Apple Crisp 97	Prune Whip 109
Apple Goodie 96	Pudding Dessert 97
Baked Cracker Pudding 101	Pumpkin Log 113
Caramel Dumplings 106	Pumpkin Roll 113
Cheese Cake 112	Quick Baked Apples 108
Cherry Delight 100	Raspberry Special 99
Chocolate Cheesecake 109	Road To Heaven Dessert 97
Chocolate Lovers Dessert 95	Strawberry Swirl Dessert 99
Chocolate Pudding Dessert 95	Try Pudding Dessert 94

Twinkie Pudding 100
Velvety Orange Ice Cream 115

Cakes and Frostings 119
Angel Food Cake 127
Apple Cake 135
Apple Nut Cake 135
Better Cake Mix 122
Blackberry Cake 120
Blueberry Bruckle Coffee Cake .. 131
Butter Cream Frosting 141
Cake Dessert 125
Caramel Icing 140
Carrot Cake 138
Carrot Pineapple Bundt Cake 137
Cherry Coffee Cake 131
Chiffon Cake 124
Chocolate Chip Cake 122
Cinnamon Pecan Coffee Cake ... 132
Cool Whip Frosting 141
Crazy Cake 124
Cream Cheese Frosting 141
Cream Filled Coffee Cake 132
Creamy Chocolate Frosting 141
Fluffy Lemon Frosting 142
Fluffy White Icing 140
Ho Ho Cake 121
Hot Milk Cake 123
Johnny Cake 120
Lazy Daisy Cake 130
Lemon Cake 140
Lemon-Lime Refrigerator Cake ... 139
Miriacle Whip Cake 121
Moist Chocolate Cake 135, 136
Oatmeal Cake 129
Old Fashioned Chocolate Cake .. 125
Old Fashioned Hickory
    Nut Cake 126
Pineapple Nut Cake 136
Pineapple Upside Down Cake .. 136
Peach Cake 120
Pound Cake 129
Pumpkin Cake Bars 127
Pumpkin Upside-Down Cake 125
Quick Gingerbread 128
Royal Sunshine Cake 124
Salad Dressing Cake 123

Solomon Cake 120
Sour Cream Coffee Cake 133
Springtime Chocolate Cake 122
Strawberry Frosting 141
Strawberry Shortcake 126
Sugar N' Spice Carrot Cake 139
Texas Sheet Cake 133, 134
Turtle Cake 121
Walnut Wonder Coffee Cake 130
White Cake 137, 138
White Texas Sheet Cake 134
White Crisco Icing 140
Wonder Wonder Coffee Cake 131
Yummy Cake 123
Zucchini Cupcakes 128

Pies 145
Abby's Famous Pecan Pie 155
Blueberry Cream Pie 152
Candy Bar Pie 157
Chonie Pie 161
Coconut Cream Pie 159
Cool N' Easy Easter Pie 161
Creamy Chocolate Layered Pie ... 157
Custard Pie 154
Double Layer Pumpkin Pie 154
Dried Apples 149
Dutch Chocolate Pie 156
Filling for Raspberry, Blackberry,
    Strawberry, or Blueberry Pie .. 146
Frozen Mint Pie 161
"Granny's" Apple Pie 149
Golden Apple Bundles 150
Half Moon Pies 150
Happiness Pie 152
Impossible Cherry Pie 151
Key Lime Pie 160
Lemon Pie 156
Lemon Mocha Pie 156
Lemon Sponge Pie 155
Malt Ball Pie 157
Million Dollar Pie 160
Mince Meat Pie Filling 147
Never Fail Pie Dough 146
Oatmeal Pie 153
Pastry 146
Peach Pie 147, 148

Peachy Peach Pie 148
Peanut Butter Pie 158
Peanut Butter Cream Pie 158
Peanut Butter Cup Pie 159
Pecan Pie 155
Perfect Meringue 147
Pumpkin Pie 154
Raisin Pie 152
Rhubarb Pie 153
Rice Krispy Pie 160
Snitz Pie 149
Sour Cream Apple Pie 148
Sour Cream Rhubarb Pie 153
Strawberry Pie 151
Strawberry Chiffon Pie 151
Vanilla Crumb Pie 153

Cookies 165
Apple Cheese Bars 174
Best Sugar Cookies
   Under Heaven 183
Buttermilk Cookies 184
Buttermilk Chocolate Bars 177
Butterscotch Cookies 179
Butterscotch Drop Cookies 180
Chewy Brownie Cookies 191
Christmas Cut-outs Cookies 193
Chocolate Caramel Bars 174
Chocolate Chip Bars 192
Chocolate Chip Cookies ... 190, 191
Chocolate Marshmallow
   Cookies 170
Chocolate Mint Brownies 166
Chocolate Mint Sugar Cookies .. 167
Chocolate Nut Cookies 167
Chocolate Pixies 185
Classic Chocolate Chip Cookies .. 190
Coffee Cake Cookies 181
Cream Cheese Bars 179
Cream Wafers 182
Date Filled Cookies 183
Debbie Cookies 171
Delicious Bars 176
Double Chocolate Chip
   Cookies 190
Double Chocolate Crunch Bars 168
Easy Lemon Cookies 176

Everything Cookies 169
Forgotten Cookies 173
Fudge-nut Bars 175
Honey Cookies 188
Irresistable Peanut Butter
   Cookies 172
Jello Cookies 170
Lemon Bars 176
Maple Leaf Cookies 182
Marble Squares 179
Mexican Wedding Cakes 192
Molasses Cookies 187
Monster Cookies 184
No Bake Chocolate Oatmeal
   Cookies 168
Oatmeal Cookies 173
Oh Henry Bars 177
One Bowl Brownies 166
Orange Cookies 189
Oreo Cookies 168
Outrageous Chocolate Chip
   Cookies 189
Party M & M Cookies 184
Peanut Butter Blossoms 181
Peanut Butter Chocolate Bars 175
Peanut Butter Fingers 172
Peanut Butter Oatmeal Cookies 172
Pecan Puffs 192
Potato Chip Cookies 169
Pumpkin Bars 186
Pumpkin Whoopie Pie Cookies .. 186
Raisin Cookies 187
Raisin Top Cookies 187
Raspberry Bars 179
Rebel Bars 178
Reese's Chewy Chocolate
   Pan Cookies 177
Soft Ginger Cookies 188
Seven Layer Bars 178
Soft Molasses Cookies 188
Soft Sugar Cookies 183
Sour Cream Raisin Bars 186
Spell Binders 182
Surprise Bars 178
Thumb Print Cookies 192
Triple Treat Cookies 169
Twinkies 173

White Chocolate Cookies 180
Whoopie Cookies 185
Whoopie Pies 185
Valentine Butter Cookies 193

Snacks and Misc. 197
Amish Church Peanut Butter 205
Apple Butter 205
Best Big Batch Tomato
    Sauce (to can) 207
Caramel Corn 200
Chicken in a Biscuit Crackers 202
Chocolate Marshmallow Sauce ... 206
Cinnamon Popcorn 200
Coconut Bird Nests 201
Cool Whip Treat 203
Corn Salad 207
Crispy Caramel Corn 200
Fantasy Fudge 203
Finger Jello 199
Fish Batter 206
Fudge Bars 204
Good Pickles 205
Joggin' in a Jug 206
Party Mix 202
Peachy Orange Jam 204
Peanut Brittle 201
Peanut Butter Candy Cookies 201
Peanut Butter Sandwich Spread 205
Pinwheel Finger Jello 199
Puppy Chow 202
Quick Strawberry Jam 204
Rice Krispie Treats 202
Reese's Temptations 203
Smore's 201
Soft Pretzels 198
Strawberry Jam 204
Sweet Dill Pickles 206
Vegetable Bars 198
Vegetable Pizza 198
White Sauce 207
Yogurt 206

Favorite Recipes from the Heart of Amish Country

Rachel Miller
862 SR 93 NW
Sugarcreek, Ohio 44681

Please send _____ copies   @ $9.95 each $ _____
                              including tax
Postage and handling   @ $2.00 each $ _____
                                   TOTAL $ _____

Name _____
Address _____
City _____ State _____ Zip _____

Make checks payable to Rachel Miller

- -

Favorite Recipes from the Heart of Amish Country

Rachel Miller
862 SR 93 NW
Sugarcreek, Ohio 44681

Please send _____ copies   @ $9.95 each $ _____
                              including tax
Postage and handling   @ $2.00 each $ _____
                                   TOTAL $ _____

Name _____
Address _____
City _____ State _____ Zip _____

Make checks payable to Rachel Miller